The Raybestos Brakettes, Connecticut Falc
changers in women's softball!
Tony Renzoni's book highlights some of the greatest sport icons in the sporting world. But, equally important, Renzoni points out the impact that these women athletes have had in raising the bar for all females. His book reveals how women can truly compete, despite major obstacles and all the critics and skeptics they have encountered throughout the years.
Both of these teams were highly competitive and exciting to watch.
The Brakettes and Falcons are an integral component of the history of women in sport—and in life!
I highly recommend this book to all sports fans!
—Hall of famer Carol Hutchins, winningest head coach in NCAA Division I Softball history

. . . . . .

An important central theme of Tony Renzoni's book is softball's positive influence on young girls and women. In Connecticut's Girls of Summer, *you will hear the stories of many of the extraordinary athletes who were part of these teams, as well as their advice to young girls who dream of excelling in the world of fast-pitch softball. I invite all of you to share in the pride and satisfaction of Connecticut's most historic and preeminent sports franchises.*
As an advocate of women in sports, I highly recommend this uplifting book to all sports fans!
—Ann Liguori, sports talk show host, WFAN; owner/executive producer/host, Sports Innerview *cable series; author*

. . . . . .

The success of the Connecticut Falcons and the Raybestos Brakettes influenced generations of young women.
When my sister Joan first started playing, the options were very limited for females in sports. Teams like the Brakettes opened the door for girls to get involved and play at a young age. The Connecticut Falcons team was instrumental in highlighting female athletes on the world stage. The Falcons dominated the International Women's Professional Softball League for the entire four years of its existence. Being able to see these accomplished players on the field was inspiring to all girls wanting to join a women's softball team.

In his book Connecticut's Girls of Summer: The Brakettes and the Falcons, *Tony Renzoni highlights how these two incredible teams shaped the landscape of women's sports, not just in Connecticut, but all over the world. I highly recommend this tribute for anyone looking to learn about the contributions of these two amazing Connecticut organizations.*
—*Joe Joyce, brother of hall of fame great Joan Joyce*

. . . . . .

Throughout their illustrious history, the Brakettes were successful because they worked extremely hard to embrace many adversarial conditions with grace, dignity and a little humor. They have always been taught the great balance and understanding of striving to be their personal best while at the same time mastering the skill of being a great teammate. The legacy of the Brakettes teams is their ability to succeed at a very high level and thrive in this sport as true competitors, as champions, and with the common goal of always putting the team first. This combination proved to be the secret to winning.
Tony Renzoni's book Connecticut's Girls of Summer: The Brakettes and the Falcons *pays homage to all the very talented athletes who had the good fortune of playing for these two outstanding teams.*
I strongly recommend this book to ALL softball fans (and sports fans in general)!
—*Amber Radomski (Morgan), Brakettes*

. . . . . .

I have been associated with the Brakettes for over seventy-five years as a fan, coach and manager. It has, indeed, been my distinct pleasure and honor to be associated with so many very talented athletes and wonderful people!
In his book Connecticut's Girls of Summer: The Brakettes and the Falcons, *Tony Renzoni not only discusses the unparalleled success of both these teams but also includes detailed accounts and fun experiences shared by many former players—in their own words. All sports fans, especially softball fans, will thoroughly enjoy this book.*
Strongly recommended!
—*John Stratton, legendary Brakettes manager*

. . . . . .

The story of women's fast-pitch softball is a unique and fascinating chapter in Connecticut's very rich sports history. Tony Renzoni's book Connecticut's Girls of Summer: The Brakettes and the Falcons *is required reading for anyone who wants to learn about these two incredible teams or relive that golden age.*
—Paul Pacelli, talk show host, WICC-600 AM/107.3 FM

• • • • • •

In 2022, we celebrated the fiftieth anniversary of Title IX, which guaranteed equitable athletic opportunities for girls and women in sports.
Tony Renzoni's book Connecticut's Girls of Summer: The Brakettes and the Falcons *gives the historical facts about great softball players and coaches who paved the way for today's aspiring athletes well before the passage of Title IX.*
These leaders were nationally and internationally accomplished coaches and players who many of today's softball leaders and student-athletes can look up to and thank for paving the way for today's vast softball opportunities.
This book is highly recommended to all sports fans everywhere!
—Debbie Chin, retired associate vice president and director of athletics, University of New Haven

• • • • • •

The pioneers of fast-pitch softball have passed on a well-lit torch! It is important to note that today's players stand on the shoulders of all these very talented pioneers!
Our Brakettes team members realized the unique opportunity we had that most females didn't experience in sports during that era. We developed a deep respect for the game, for our sponsor, for the Brakettes who had gone before us, for our teammates and for our top-level competition.
As Tony Renzoni points out in his well-researched book Connecticut's Girls of Summer: The Brakettes and the Falcons, *the game of softball has had a very positive impact on many girls and women throughout the years, not only as a sport, but also in life.*
I highly recommend this book!
—Peggy Kellers, Brakettes, National Softball Hall of Fame

Published by The History Press
Charleston, SC
www.historypress.com

First published 2023

Manufactured in the United States

ISBN 9781467154192

Library of Congress Control Number: 2022951605

Connecticut's
GIRLS OF SUMMER

THE BRAKETTES AND THE FALCONS

TONY RENZONI

FOREWORD BY DONNA LOPIANO, NATIONAL SOFTBALL HALL OF FAME

AFTERWORD BY MICHELE SMITH, OLYMPIC GOLD MEDALIST
AND ESPN COMMENTATOR

THE
History
PRESS

Joan Joyce and the author. *Photo by Kathy Gage.*

This book is dedicated to Joan Joyce—an outstanding athlete,
coach and a very dear friend.
On March 26, 2022, the world lost a true legend
when Joan Joyce passed away at age eighty-one.
Rest in peace, Joanie.
Love, Tony

CONTENTS

CONTENTS

ONCE UPON A TIME

Once upon a time, girls who played sports were neither revered nor celebrated. Even the term *tomboy* was used in a derogatory manner. The ban on women participating in the male-dominated sport of baseball was just one example of the discrimination that existed.

However, there was a special place that existed for many girls and women at that time—the proverbial "field of dreams"—where thousands of people came to watch. That place was women's fast-pitch softball. And the most celebrated of all the fast-pitch softball teams was the legendary Raybestos Brakettes. Local newspapers such as the *Bridgeport Post* celebrated the exploits of these female softball athletes on the front page of the sports section, next to coverage of the New York Yankees or the Boston Red Sox. In the case of the Brakettes, the games were played at night under brilliant lights, with thousands of fans applauding every strikeout, base hit and extraordinary defensive play. Children, in droves, lined up for autographs of their favorite players—some who were superstars, the equals of Mickey Mantle or Ted Williams.

Softball player Joan Joyce was one such female superstar, an incredibly gifted pitcher for the Brakettes, a team that became perennial national softball champions. Their town—Stratford, Connecticut—and Raybestos Memorial Field became their field of dreams. Newspapers in Connecticut as well as in other parts of the country treated these extremely talented Brakettes with coverage and adulation equal to that afforded major league baseball players of the day. Joyce was an extraordinary multisport athlete—a softball pitcher, a USA national basketball team star, a LPGA golfer, a volleyball star—a multidimensional athlete with no equal, the likes of which we may never see again. Indeed, Joan's exploits as an athlete and the success of the Raybestos Brakettes were legendary, but that was not the whole story.

As is the case with heroes like Joan and many other Brakettes, boys and girls wanted to be like them, aspiring to be among those whose competencies were universally respected—not in a selfish sense but because all humans wish to be treated with respect and appreciation. These glimpses of greatness, often created in competitive sport by individual athletes and teams, become indelibly burned into the memory of observers. Children pursue sports to "be like a Brakette" or "be like Joan" and in doing so become exposed to how a person becomes competent at a chosen task—the repetition, attention to detail and intense training. And as each young sportsperson grows older and discovers other personal interests and talents, the lessons of the hero become applicable—tenacity, incredible competitiveness, hard work, attention to detail and being part of and the leader of a team. The hero's influence is never limited to those who pursue athletics as their life focus.

Connecticut's Girls of Summer: The Brakettes and the Falcons is about the impact of softball and its female heroes on the lives of all girls and women. This is a story of the alignment of charismatic leaders, female athletes and special communities across the country that together laid the groundwork that eventually led to the passage of the historic Title IX law. Women are now afforded the opportunity to actively participate in a myriad of educational opportunities (admission to graduate programs in medicine, law, engineering, coaching, sportscasting, etc.).

I had the distinct honor of playing alongside my hero Joan Joyce as well as many other very talented athletes when I pitched for the Raybestos Brakettes softball team. Actually, Joan and I were also teammates on the Connecticut Clippers Volleyball team (along with Debbie Chin and the Brakettes' Brenda Reilly and Lou Albrecht) and the Raybestos Basketball team (which included Brakettes Ann DeLuca, Brenda Reilly and Willie Roze).

Being inducted into the National Softball Hall of Fame as well as the Connecticut Hall of Fame were two especially important honors for me.

My career in softball, as well as in other sports, taught me many valuable life lessons—lessons I will always cherish.

Donna A. Lopiano, PhD
National Softball Hall of Fame inductee
President, Sports Management Resources
Adjunct Professor of Sports Management, SCSU
Former CEO, Women's Sports Foundation

ACKNOWLEDGEMENTS

Thanks to: Colleen Renzoni, Dr. Kerry Renzoni, Sir Bronn, Amber Radomski Morgan, Ann Liguori, Bev Mulonet Hollis, Bill Rienzi, Billie Jean King, Bridget Joyce Wright, Carol Hutchins, Carol Spanks, Christina Sutcliff, Danielle Henderson, Debbie Chin, Denise Denis, Diane Schumacher, Donna Lopiano, Fran Santoli, Harlan Gage, Irene Shea, Jackie Ledbetter, Jane Blalock, Janice Nelson, Joan Joyce, Joe Joyce Jr., Janis Joyce, Joe and Mary Blacker, John Stratton, Joyce Compton, Kaci Clark Zerbe, Kaitlyn Dugan, Kathy Strahan, Kristine Botto Drust, Linda Finelli, Margie Wright, Marty Morra, Max Voorhess, Meghan Joyce Bolesta, Michele Smith, Pat Harrison, Pat Serafin, Patti Schippani, Paul Pacelli, Peggy Kellers, Shane Dugan, Shirley Topley, Stormy Irwin, Tatum Buckley and Willie Roze.

A special thank-you to Kathy Gage, Mary Lou Pennington and Ken Evans for all your assistance with many photos in this book. And also a big thank-you to my two outstanding editors: Mike Kinsella and Abigail Fleming.

INTRODUCTION

The sport of softball is a microcosm of life. Those who succeed and thrive in this sport are true competitors, with a great balance and an understanding of striving to be their best, while handling their failures with grace, dignity and a little humor. Their successes on the field directly translate to their abilities to succeed in life.
—Amber (Radomski) Morgan, Brakettes

This is a book about the game of softball—specifically, women's fast-pitch softball. More importantly, it is about the game of life. As Amber (Radomski) Morgan asserted, "The sport of softball is a microcosm of life." Softball encapsulates much of what life is all about. The sport runs the gamut of winning, losing, heroism, hardships, teamwork, fun, risk-taking, overcoming challenges and always striving to be the best.

Nowhere is this more evident than in the struggles and obstacles faced by women in their quest to even the playing field in a sport they love—softball. Keep in mind that women were faced with the indignity of being banned from baseball because it was thought to be "too strenuous" a sport for female players. But the notion of baseball being too tough for women never was put to a real test. Instead, this was the thinking and the feeling for many years by such male baseball commissioners as Kenesaw Mountain Landis and Ford Frick.

It has been ingrained in us for so long now that maybe many people have come to the realization that women could not possibly compete with men in baseball. But I can't help but think that my dear friend Joan Joyce, if given the opportunity, would have somehow worked her way into becoming a better-than-average baseball player—most likely not at a star level and maybe only a semipro player, but I am convinced Joan would have found a way to compete. Joanie was the most confident person I have ever known when it came to her participation in sports. If anyone could have done it, it would have been someone like Joanie. There were other female athletes who, if given the chance, could have made a name for themselves (and therefore for women in general) in the sport of baseball. But we may never know.

So, taking what life had to offer, women turned to the sport of softball.

The path to excellence that every women's softball team strives for can certainly be found in the two legendary teams highlighted in this book: the Brakettes and the Connecticut Falcons.

In their seventy-six-year history, the Brakettes of Stratford, Connecticut, are considered the most successful and longest-running organized women's sports franchise of all time. Among their many other accomplishments, the Brakettes' forty National Championships serve as the gold standard of excellence. Likewise, the Connecticut Falcons, by all measures, were certainly the most dominant pro women's team in the four-year existence of the Women's Profession Softball League (WPS).

But more important than the incredible success of these two teams is how they achieved their success and the manner in which they presented themselves in their path to excellence. Both teams worked hard and had to overcome many obstacles in their yearly quest to attain the championship title. But both teams did so with an understanding of the importance of teamwork, an immense pride, a respect for their opposition and having fun all the way. All the players I spoke with and interviewed made it clear that they truly loved playing fast-pitch softball despite receiving little or no compensation and shared a common desire that players following in their footsteps share this same love of the game.

The pioneers of fast-pitch softball (of all teams) look back with fondness and share a sense of pride that they were the ones who have made it possible for girls and women today to be a part of the great game of softball. As one pioneer put it, "The women softball players today stand on the shoulders of all of us pioneers of the sport."

My goal is for all readers to come away with an understanding of the effect that softball has had on so many women and girls throughout the years, not only the sport but also the important role that softball has played in their lives.

Women's softball is, indeed, a microcosm of life.

Author's Note I urge all readers to pay particular attention to the chapters "Recollections: What Softball Means to Me" and "Players' Advice to Young Girls (and Women) Who Would Like to Excel in Fast-Pitch Softball."

I found the responses from these former softball players to be enlightening.

1

BILL SIMPSON'S DREAM

Bill Simpson's efforts put softball on the map in Connecticut and made the Raybestos Brakettes (and Raybestos Cardinals) household names to softball fans everywhere. Simpson made Stratford, Connecticut, the Mecca of women's and men's fast-pitch softball.
—National Softball Hall of Fame, 1976

Everything associated with the Brakettes was first class thanks to the generous sponsorship of Bill Simpson and the Brakettes organization. Mr. Simpson covered our travel, meal allowance and compensation for time off from work when we played our games. Because of this, I felt that I had won the lottery!
—Pat Harrison, Brakettes

Bill Simpson casually took one of his coaches aside and said, "We're getting close, very close. Our girls are very talented, but they are still very young. The only thing missing is a proven champion that can help get the girls to the National Championship. I think I found just the player for that." With that, Bill Simpson showed the coach a 1955 article in a California newspaper with the headline "Pitching Sensation Leads Team to 4th Championship Title." Simpson went on to say, "I actually saw her pitch back in 1953 in San Antonio, Texas, and she is amazing. If we can somehow persuade this player to join our team, I believe we will be on our way to a championship title."

William "Bill" Simpson was a visionary. As the general manager and sponsor of the Raybestos Company in his hometown of Stratford, Connecticut, Simpson organized both the company-sponsored women's softball team (the Raybestos Brakettes) and the men's softball team (the Raybestos Cardinals).

Bill Simpson. *Courtesy of Brakettes Photo Archive.*

Simpson was known for his absolute support of his teams and players (women and men) and determination to provide top-notch softball teams for the fans in his hometown of Stratford. He was also a man of great generosity, providing all the support and financial backing needed for his teams. He even sponsored dinners and trips for his teams after winning championships and other such accomplishments. Janice Nelson (Bertha Ragan Tickey's daughter) fondly remembers Bill Simpson:

> *Mr. Simpson was a really quiet, unassuming and humble man. A very down-to-earth, generous person who loved the sport of softball. I remember that when he picked up my mom and me at Idlewild Airport (now JFK), he drove us to Connecticut in an old Mercury car. One of the back doors of the car was actually tied together with wire. Here was this man who owned Raybestos and was able to purchase any car he wanted, but was just satisfied driving his old used car. He much preferred spending his money on others, especially team members of both his softball teams.*
>
> *Mr. Simpson would walk through his Raybestos plant and made a point to stop and chat with all his employees. He knew the names of all of his workers there. When one of his employees became ill, he would send a driver to the person's house to purchase groceries or any other items for the family. The Raybestos' employees and team members were like his family. And so, my mom became part of his family, which was one of the reasons why my mother decided to join his Raybestos Brakettes team.*

Simpson already had a men's championship team—the Raybestos Cardinals. But Bill's heart and soul was mainly focused on creating a perennial women's championship team. Such thinking was almost unheard of in those days. Sure, his women's team would play on an amateur level, but the competition was stiff and there was a great deal of softball talent— so much so, Simpson had high hopes for his women's teams. Despite the naysayers, Bill was determined. He envisioned a women's softball team in the image of the New York Yankees (twenty-seven championships) or the Montreal Canadiens (twenty-five championships).

Beginning in 1945, the young ladies who worked at Simpson's Raybestos plant formed their own softball teams (they also formed a non-sponsored basketball team). Despite the fact that the softball teams were not yet sponsored by the company, these teams did fairly well. For example, the 1946 women's team earned city and state titles. All this changed in 1947, when Simpson formally sponsored his first women's softball club. He named his first team the Raybestos Girls All-Stars. In 1948, the tag Girls All-Stars was dropped, and the team was officially known as the Raybestos Brakettes (the name was a reference to the company, which produced brake linings for automobiles and trucks). With an 18-2 record, the 1948 team captured the Eastern Coast Women's Softball Championship.

Simpson was aware of some of the talented women who worked at his Raybestos plant and played on his team. But would that be enough to form a dominant women's softball team as he envisioned? In the earlier years, his Brakettes teams fared well and even made it to the National Women's ASA Softball Tournament, only to see his team fall short of their goal of

Rare 1945 photo of future Brakettes at a top-notch restaurant to celebrate their performance in a non-sponsored tournament. Dinner was paid for by Bill Simpson. *Left to right*: Betty Springer, Tina Primavera, Mary Baker, Doris Davis, Janet Wick, Mary Primavera and Marge Gowing. *Courtesy of Brakettes Photo Archive.*

Brakettes owner and general manager Bill Simpson (*standing, fourth from right*) treated his team to a two-day stay in Las Vegas after winning the national championship. Pictured here are 1958 Brakettes championship heroes Joan Joyce (*seated third from left*) and Mary Hartman (*standing second from right*). *Courtesy of Brakettes Photo Archive.*

Bill Simpson with several Brakettes. *Courtesy of Brakettes Photo Archive.*

Left to right: Bertha Tickey, Joan Joyce, Bill Simpson and his wife and Micki Stratton. *Courtesy of Janis Joyce (sister of Joan Joyce).*

becoming national champions. The players he assembled for his teams possessed a great deal of talent on the field. However, in his mind, Bill was convinced that there was one key ingredient missing, which he summed up in one word: *confidence*.

Bill Simpson instinctively knew what must be done, and he would pull out all the stops to reach his goal. In order for his Brakettes to become a championship team, he must make every effort to entice one special player to join his fifteen-year-old pitching phenom Joan Joyce and the rest of his Raybestos Brakettes team.

That player was the Orange Lionettes' star thirty-three-year-old pitcher: Bertha Ragan.

2

"BLAZING" BERTHA ARRIVES

My mother, Bertha, would come home from a day at the office, put on her apron, and fix dinner for herself, my dad and me. Once dishes were done, she would immediately grab her ball bag, filled with glove, balls and cleats, and then head off to a practice or a game. Her teammates were such a joyful source of camaraderie. Bertha loved her sport and the competition it brought. Always seeking a higher level of play, she arrived as a Brakette—and was a champion. I consider her even more as a champion mom!
—Janice Ragan Nelson, daughter of Bertha Ragan Tickey

Born Borica Petinak (March 1923) in Orosi, California, Bertha Ragan was the fifth of seven children of Chetko and Andja Petinak, Serbian immigrants from Bosnia and Herzegovina.

Bertha began her career as a shortstop on the Sultana girls' softball travel ball team in the mid-1930s. She then became the pitcher for the Alta Chevrolet team in Dinuba, California, in 1937.

In 1939, at age sixteen, Bertha joined the Orange Lionettes softball team in Southern California. It was there that she became a superstar and fan favorite. Bertha led the Lionettes to the National Women's ASA Softball Championships in 1950, 1951, 1952 and 1955. She became known as "Blazing Bertha" and quickly became a local legend.

Three thousand miles away, Bill Simpson (the Brakettes general manager) followed Bertha's heroics closely. Simpson was aware of her amazing accomplishments with the Lionettes. He was mainly interested in Bertha's

Bertha Ragan with daughter Janice arriving in Connecticut to play for the Raybestos Brakettes. *Courtesy of Janice Nelson.*

winning attitude, mental toughness and the confidence she conveyed to her teammates. This is exactly what Simpson felt was missing from his women's softball team. He truly believed that his squad was a talented team and was proud of the fact that they competed in national tournaments. But, knowing they were very young, he felt there was something important that was missing, some intangible qualities—confidence and a belief in themselves.

Bill Simpson was sure that Bertha Ragan was the final piece of the puzzle to finally make his Brakettes the national softball champions. She was the missing ingredient he was looking for. And he was right.

And so, Bill Simpson pulled out all the stops (and resources) to encourage Bertha to leave California and join the Raybestos Brakettes. It was a tough sell for Simpson and not an easy decision for Bertha. Leaving the Lionettes team and the fans (which she truly loved) in order to join a Connecticut team that had not yet won a championship required a lot of soul searching. It would also mean leaving the beautiful California weather. And there was one other important factor. Bertha had a thirteen-year-old daughter (Janice) who would need a lot of convincing to leave her friends and classmates in California. Bertha's love for Janice was top priority. So, an arrangement was made whereby Simpson agreed to have Bertha and Janice fly back to California once the season ended so Janice would be able to continue to attend school there. To sweeten the pot, Simpson agreed to have Bertha's Lionettes catcher, Joan Kammeyer, join the Brakettes to team up with Ragan. Simpson would pay for Kammeyer's travel expenses. While in Connecticut, Bertha would work at Simpson's Raybestos plant and live in a nice beach house. Once the logistics were worked out, an agreement was finally reached, and Bertha agreed to become a member of the Raybestos Brakettes.

Bertha Petinak
Alta Chevrolet Girls
1937
Dinuba, California

Right: Bertha Ragan, 1937. *Courtesy of Janice Nelson*.

Below, left to right: Bertha Ragan, Donna Hebert and Joan Joyce, 1956. *Courtesy of Janice Nelson*.

Bertha Ragan was known for accepting a challenge, and she became convinced that she could help the Brakettes reach the national finals and win the elusive championship title. Even before she put on a Brakette uniform, the rumors swiftly began to circulate in and around the Stratford area. The headline in the February edition of the local newspaper (the *Bridgeport Post*) gave fuel to these rumors with the headline "Women's Pitching Ace Might Join Brakettes." Sharing the same feeling of the Brakettes general manager, the Stratford residents believed that if these rumors were true, this could be the key ingredient needed for their beloved Brakettes team to finally become a national championship team.

In 1956, Bertha packed up and headed to Connecticut to help Bill Simpson develop his Raybestos Brakettes into a world-class team. As a member of the Brakettes, Bertha Ragan helped the team win national championships in 1958, 1959, 1960, 1963, 1966, 1967 and 1968.

During this amazing run of championship seasons, Bertha found the time in 1963 to marry Ed Tickey, a catcher for the Raybestos Cardinals men's softball team.

And so, Bertha Ragan Tickey, together with fifteen-year-old Waterbury pitching phenom Joan Joyce, set the stage for what would become a women's fast-pitch softball worldwide sensation—the Brakettes dynasty.

Praise for Bertha Ragan Tickey

When Bertha joined the Brakettes, she changed the whole complexion of the team. She was so good. She changed everything not by words but by her actions. We began to really believe in ourselves, and our team became very competitive. Bertha led by example. I was only fifteen years old, but I was certainly influenced by Bertha's winning attitude.
—Joan Joyce

A true test of greatness is consistency over a period of time, even under the most adverse conditions. Pitcher Bertha Ragan Tickey certainly met that criteria during a legendary career covering almost three decades.
—National Softball Hall of Fame

3

1958

The Brakettes Dynasty Begins

As Hartman raced around third base heading for home, the stadium shook with a thunderous applause from the Brakettes fans. Hartman's dramatic, inside-the-park home run gave the Brakettes a slim 1–0 lead. The Brakettes, behind Joan Joyce's amazing no-hitter and Mary Hartman's "storybook" home run, won their first national championship.
—excerpt from the book Connecticut Softball Legend Joan Joyce

O nce Bertha Ragan joined the Brakettes in 1956, Bill Simpson felt confident that he had now assembled a team that would finally bring the national championship title to his home state of Connecticut. And his dream would soon be realized.

In what became locally known as "The Big Out," the young and gritty Brakettes catcher Micki Macchietto made an outstanding defensive play in the 1956 North Atlantic Regional Championship game. This play proved significant in Brakettes history. In this regional championship game, the Brakettes were protecting a narrow lead against the powerful defending champions—the Caggiano team of Massachusetts. Macchietto fearlessly blocked home plate, thwarting the opponent's attempt to tie the score (and perhaps go ahead). Micki's brilliant defensive play enabled the Brakettes to win the game and qualify for the 1956 Women's National Tournament. The Brakettes finished fourth in the national tournament. This was no small feat; 1956 was the year that the Brakettes finally proved to the league (and to themselves) that they were a championship-quality team. Two years later, the Brakettes would finally become national champions.

Captain Mary Hartman along with Coach Al Martin and Manager Vin Cullen watch the Brakettes work out on August 24, 1958, six days prior to the championship tournament. *Courtesy of Brakettes Photo Archive.*

The year 1958 marked the beginning of the Brakettes dynasty. It was the year that the Brakettes won their first national championship title. But winning that first national championship wasn't easy. It took a heroic last-inning home run and the emergence of a teenage phenom to capture the elusive championship title. It would be the first of many championships for the Brakettes.

The 1958 Women's Softball National Championship was held at Raybestos Field in Stratford from August 30, 1958, to September 5, 1958. The championship game of 1958 pitted the defending champion, Fresno Rockets, against the upstart Raybestos Brakettes of Stratford, Connecticut.

On Friday September 5, 1958, the Brakettes were locked in a major struggle with California's Fresno Rockets in the final and deciding game of the Women's Softball National Championship. The championship game was played in front of an overflow crowd of fifteen thousand fans at Raybestos Memorial Field. The Fresno Rockets were a powerful team and three-time national champions who were defending their 1957 championship. The Brakettes, however, felt good about their chances of winning the championship mainly because they had their ace pitcher, "Blazing Bertha" Ragan, on the mound.

In the top of the third inning, with the score knotted at 0–0, Ragan ran off the mound to field a bunt by Fresno's Dot Stolze and severely sprained a muscle in her hip. The injury was so bad that Ragan had to be rushed to nearby Bridgeport Hospital. The players and the fans were stunned. Suddenly, panic set in. A decision had to be made as to who would relieve Ragan. But who could be counted on to handle such a high-pressure situation? Enter Joan Joyce.

The teenage Joan Joyce was called in from first base to the pitching mound. As Joan told it, "The coach put his arm around me and said, 'Go in and just do the best you can.' Do the best I can? To beat the Rockets, I knew I could not give up a run." It was a logical choice by the coach; four days earlier, Joyce pitched a no-hitter against a Detroit team in her only previous tournament start. However, Joan had never pitched in a national championship game with all the pressure associated with a deciding match-up.

The hope was that Joyce would keep the game close until the Brakettes' bats came alive. In the game's first two innings, the Rockets were hitless but saw their opportunity batting against this young "kid" who had only turned eighteen two weeks prior to the game. Undaunted, Joyce retired the first ten batters she faced, including seven strikeouts. The next batter (Terry Urrutia) became the lone Fresno batter to reach base off Joyce when she walked with two outs in the sixth inning. Joyce then retired the next Fresno batter (Marylin Sypriano) to end the sixth.

The Rockets' hitters were completely baffled by the power and accuracy of Joyce's slingshot delivery.

Despite Joan's brilliant pitching going into the final seventh inning, the Brakettes were still without a run. As Joan explained, "Knowing my stuff was really good that game, I walked into the dugout and told my teammates, 'Just get me a run and I will take it from there.'"

And so, as the seventh and final inning approached and with the score still deadlocked at 0–0, Brakettes team captain Mary Hartman stepped up to the plate. Heeding Joan's advice, Mary knew that she had to get things going if the Brakettes were going to score that run that Joan needed. With two strikes called against her, Hartman finally got the pitch she was looking for. With that, Mary drove the ball deep into the right field corner. As Hartman raced around third base heading for home, the stadium shook with a thunderous applause from the Brakettes fans. Hartman's dramatic "storybook" inside-the-park home run gave the Brakettes a slim 1–0 lead.

Having gotten the run she needed, now it was up to Joan Joyce to make the 1–0 score stand. But it wasn't going to be easy.

In the bottom of the seventh and final inning, Joyce had the monumental task of facing the potent heart of the Rockets squad in a tense situation: first baseman Gloria May and future hall of famers catcher Kay Rich and third baseman Jeanne Contel. It was then that the Brakettes fans got their first glimpse of two of Joan's traits that would endure throughout her career: confidence and determination. Undeterred by the difficult task ahead, Joan promptly went to work. Joyce got May to ground weakly to second baseman Brenda Reilly for the first out. She then struck out Kay Rich. Finally, Contel drove a ball deep to center field, and Edna Fraser caught the ball at the center field fence for the third and final out. The Brakettes, behind Joyce's amazing no-hitter (and near-perfect game), won their first national championship.

Members of the powerful Fresno Rockets at tournament prior to taking the field. *Courtesy of Brakettes Photo Archive.*

Friday, September 5, 1958. A memorable inside-the-park home run by Brakettes' Mary Hartman. *Courtesy of Brakettes Photo Archive.*

Brakettes immediately upon winning the 1958 championship. *Courtesy of Brakettes Photo Archive.*

Above: Celebrating the 1958 national championship. *Courtesy of Brakettes Photo Archive.*

Left: The great Johnny Spring pitched a perfect game to win the national championship for the Raybestos Cardinals men's softball team in the same year as the Raybestos Brakettes (1958). *Author's collection.*

Brakettes Championship float, 1958. *Courtesy of Brakettes Photo Archive.*

In the 1958 championship tournament, Joan Joyce pitched two no-hitters, walking only two and striking out nineteen batters. Bertha Ragan, whose pitching throughout the contest was also outstanding, won the tournament MVP award. For their achievements, Joyce and Ragan were presented gifts from local shops such as Bridgeport's Artic Sports Shop.

Incidentally, Stratford's Raybestos Cardinals (led by the great Johnny Spring) won the men's 1958 World Championship Title. On Monday, September 22, 1958, thousands of fans lined the streets and also the municipal green in Stratford as the town celebrated the 1958 championships of both the Raybestos Brakettes and Raybestos Cardinals. Following a parade, ceremonies were held on the Stratford Green. It was noted that this was the first time in softball history that two world championship titles were won by eastern teams and the first time that two teams sponsored by one organization won world titles.

The 1958 championship sent a strong message to the rest of the women's softball league: the Raybestos Brakettes had suddenly become a dominant force in the sport of women's softball.

Also, it cannot be overlooked that the softball world had witnessed the emergence of a teenage dynamo: Joan Joyce.

4

JOAN JOYCE

From Teenage Phenom to the Greatest Female Athlete in Sports History

Joan Joyce is the greatest female athlete in sports history. Heck, she's one of the greatest athletes, period—male or female. She was the greatest because of her competitiveness, her mental composure and her athletic ability. I don't care what it was, softball, basketball, volleyball, bowling, golf (even cards and ping-pong)—she was tops in everything.
—John Stratton, Brakettes manager

Simply put: Joan Joyce is the greatest female athlete in sports history. This sentiment has been echoed by many in the sports industry, historians, teammates, rivals, journalists and fans.

In her prime, Joan was the most feared female pitcher in fast-pitch softball. She was revered by her opponents as well as her teammates. Her pitching success against several of Major League Baseball's greatest hitters and her dominant pitching against teams in other countries gave her further recognition throughout the United States and the rest of the world.

But her athletic accomplishments were not limited to the sport of softball. She was inducted into an incredible twenty-one Halls of Fame, excelling in a wide variety of sports. Joan set sports records throughout her career. For example, the golf record she set in 1982 has not been broken in over forty years! Also, she once set an AAU single game record by scoring sixty seven points in a basketball tournament game (long before the three-point shot was instituted). And, most overlooked, Joan was a supremely successful coach and referee.

Joan Joyce, Brakettes and Falcons superstar. *Courtesy of Brakettes Photo Archive.*

Joan Joyce was born and raised in Waterbury, Connecticut. She attended Webster Elementary School and Crosby High School. At the time, Waterbury was a sports-minded city. Joanie always credited Waterbury for enabling her the opportunity to participate in local team sports, especially softball and basketball. Joan would later find out that not many girls her age had those same opportunities in the towns they grew up in.

When Joan was twelve years old, she had her first experience with female discrimination in sports. Joanie loved baseball, idolizing New York Yankee centerfielder Mickey Mantle. When she was twelve, Joan's brother Joe Jr. invited her to play on his Little League team. After hitting a triple and a double on her first two at bats, she was told by an administrator in no uncertain terms, "Girls are not allowed to play in Little League." Undeterred, Joan turned to softball and played on girls' softball teams at Waterbury parks such as Fulton Park, City Mills and Town Plot park. As a preteen, she actually formed her own softball team at Fulton Park, and her team played against other girls from other parks in Waterbury.

As noted, Joanie's athletic career started at an early age. Once she learned that girls were banned from baseball, Joan joined the famed Raybestos Brakettes at the tender age of thirteen. As a young teenager, she also starred in basketball for Waterbury's Libra AA team and the respectable New London girls' basketball squad.

At a time when the sports world was dominated by male athletes, Joan stood out as an equal. Her goal in life was to be one of the best athletes, male or female. By all measures, she achieved that goal and earned a place among sports elites.

Keep in mind that Joan Joyce grew up at a time when women were banned from male-dominated sports and many professional sports. Once Joan finally became a professional fast-pitch softball player in 1976 for the Connecticut Falcons, she was just as dominant a player as she was on an amateur level. Most people who witnessed Joan's performance in all sports she was engaged in will testify that she would have done very well, indeed, if she had been allowed to play on a professional level with her male counterparts. Unfortunately, we will never know.

Over the years, certain women have achieved fame and success in individual sporting events (tennis, track and field, etc.). But Joan Joyce was a multidimensional athlete. Joan was a groundbreaking athlete whose dominance in team sports such as softball, volleyball and basketball gave rise to women who dreamed of expanding their participation in a variety of sports. Because of Joan Joyce, pitching mounds were extended by four feet in the WPS, golfers were required to hit their shots farther, golf courses were marked differently and opponents as well as teammates were inspired to play harder.

But most of all, because of Joan Joyce, boundaries were broken. Young girls growing up can now see themselves achieving fame and success as a member of a team sport and not just individual sporting events. Because of athletic pioneers like Joan Joyce, women now have the chance for identification with a team and for work opportunities as coaches, administrators or broadcasters and endorsements after their playing careers.

In terms of excellence in a diversity of sports, Joan is in an elite class, with only the legendary 1930s great Babe Didrikson (Zaharias) being mentioned in the same category. Didrikson excelled in golf, basketball and track and field. Joyce not only dominated the world of fast-pitch softball but also was a star athlete in basketball, volleyball, golf and bowling. Like Didrikson, Joan took up golf later in life. Joyce began playing golf seriously at age thirty-seven, while Babe was twenty-four when she began. And like Didrikson, Joan always believed that there was no sport that, in time, she could not excel in. But unlike Didrikson, Joan was not given the opportunity to participate in the Olympics, where she surely would have been a gold medalist star. In making a comparison between these two great athletes, one important and often overlooked fact that distinguishes Joan from Babe Didrikson is that Joan had an extremely successful thirty-four-year career as a referee, an eighteen-year career as a university golf coach and, most noteworthy, a successful and highly regarded softball coaching career—for well over sixty years!

People who had the good fortune to see Joan pitch were in awe, watching Joanie and her famed "slingshot" delivery. She would hurl the softball with such force that at the end of many of her pitches, her momentum would cause her to hop to her left toward first base. You had the sense that fans felt a bit sorry for the batters, who seemed to swing at her pitches when the ball was already in the catcher's glove. One batter after another would flail at the pitched ball, which to them must have looked like one big blur. As one frustrated batter was heard to say after batting against Joyce, "It would help if I was able to see the ball!"

Current Brakettes manager John Stratton first met Joanie in 1958, and they became close friends. John was impressed with Joanie's athletic ability right from the start. As John put it,

Joanie was a heck of an athlete. She had a fluid pitching delivery. I just loved watching Joanie play. She would make that ball move like nobody else. Riser, drop, curve and sometimes changeup. All effective and all devasting. Her riser was unhittable, and her drop would roll right off the table. I said at the time that the first time the batter would see the ball was when the catcher would throw the ball back to Joanie. The movement on her pitches was unbelievable.

At that time, the balls were not conducive to making the pitches move like that, because the balls had no real seams. But she somehow knew how to make that ball do what she wanted. And she was so accurate. Nowadays the seams of the balls make it easier to throw those pitches. But in Joanie's day, there were very little seams on the balls, and Joanie had to work very hard to make the ball move. Before every game I would put six new softballs on the ledge in the dugout. Joanie would pick up a ball and say, "This is a no-hit ball. Wait, this is a perfect game ball. Save this one for me."

John recalled a conversation he once had with Ted Williams, considered by many to be the greatest hitter in MLB history: "Ted Williams once told me that he couldn't hit any of her pitches, especially the riser and the drop. Joanie's pitches were extremely difficult for batters to hit."

John went on:

Joanie was also a great batter and a great baserunner. Joanie was fairly slow on the base paths, but she could read the play better than anyone and knew when to run. She knew whether the ball would drop in the outfield or whether it would be caught. Super baserunner with great instinct. She was a thinker. She never got thrown out. Joanie never got rattled in any sport she played—she was always in complete composure.

Joanie never thought she was better than anyone else. She was a great teammate who excelled in every sport she played. If she promoted herself, which she never did, she would be a household name throughout the United States and the rest of the world.

Perseverance and stamina were hallmarks of Joan Joyce's pitching. These trademarks were on full display on September 3, 1961, when Joan pitched three straight games—in *one* memorable day—with the championship game lasting nineteen innings.

The games were played in Normandale Park in Portland, Oregon. At stake was the national championship in which the Brakettes were defending champions and hoped to win their fourth-consecutive championship title. However, the Brakettes had dug themselves in a huge hole. In order to participate in the championship game, the Brakettes needed to win all three games in what turned out to be a triple-header that day. They needed Joan to perform the monumental feat of pitching all three games against powerful opponents.

The championship game took four hours and fifteen minutes to complete and lasted until 3:30 a.m. Joyce struck out forty batters in that nineteen-inning game.

In total, Joan pitched 33⅔-straight innings and struck out an incredible sixty-seven batters in a twelve-hour span—all in one memorable day.

Joan Joyce's gutsy performance that day was the talk of the entire softball world. Newspapers across the country hailed Joan's heroics as "one of the most gallant exhibitions in women's softball history."

Author's note: I asked Joanie how she felt after pitching 33⅔ innings in a single day, pitching until 3:30 a.m. in the championship game. Her response to me was, "Tony, when I went back to the hotel, I tried to take my uniform off. I found that I could not lift my arms above my hips. And I was so exhausted I just fell into bed, uniform and all."

Many people have said that striking out Ted Williams was probably the event that first got her the attention of sports fans. That may very well be the case, since those contests were thrilling and historic. However, it was Joanie's gutsy performance on September 3, 1961 (along with her 1958 championship-winning no-hitter), that really won the hearts and minds of her fans all over the world, especially in Connecticut.

In a few short years, Joan Joyce had become a softball legend.

During Joan's playing days, Joyce was an iconic figure throughout the United States and other countries, including China. However, the media outlets that covered sports figures like Joan were quite different than they are today. Joan did receive adequate newspaper coverage but little exposure from other media (there was no ESPN in her day). Also, Joan had absolutely no interest in promoting herself like many of her contemporaries or athletes today. Thus, Joan is not the household name in some areas of the country that she should be.

Like all the other members of the Brakettes, Joan was never paid for the sports she loved. To make ends meet, Joan needed to work full time.

For the most part, Joan was a teacher and coach, Actually, Joan's coaching career began soon after graduating from Waterbury's Crosby High School in 1958. She went on to coach at numerous local high schools and colleges. Aside from Waterbury Catholic High School, Joan was a teacher and coach at Stamford's Presentation High School, St. Mary's High School (Greenwich), Bethel High School, Bridgeport's Housatonic Community College, Brooklyn (NY) College and Waterbury's Mattatuck Community College. At these schools, she coached basketball and volleyball and, in the case of Brooklyn and Mattatuck Colleges, the girls' softball teams.

Sadly, on March 26, 2022, the world lost a true legend when Joan Joyce passed away at age eighty-one. As mentioned, there will always be women who will achieve greatness in individual sporting events, but there will never be another Joan Joyce.

Joan left an indelible mark on women's athletics. Throughout her playing and coaching career, Joan was a champion of women in sports. Joan Joyce's legacy was a major contributing factor in bringing women's athletics into the public spotlight.

Author's note: In my book *Connecticut Softball Legend Joan Joyce*, I devoted seven pages detailing Joanie's accomplishments in sports (and still I had to leave out some). For the purposes of this book, I will highlight just a few of her sports accomplishments.

In this chapter, I have listed some general overall career achievements. For a list of some of Joanie's accomplishments as a member of the Brakettes and Falcons, please see her writeups under individual Brakettes and Falcons players.

General Career Statistics for Joan Joyce

- Inducted into an astounding twenty-one halls of fame; starring at a very high level in fast-pitch softball, basketball, volleyball, golf and bowling; and served as referee, university golf coach and head coach of the Florida Atlantic University (FAU) women's softball team.
- 753-42 win-loss record.
- 150 no-hitters.
- 50 perfect games.
- Lifetime earned run average of 0.09.
- Struck out over 10,000 batters in her pitching career.
- A long and distinguished softball coaching career—over sixty years!
- A successful thirty-four-year career as a highly regarded basketball referee. She officiated several CIAC State Tournament games and three college national championship games.
- An eighteen-year career as a college head golf coach (FAU).
- Struck out hall of famer Ted Williams on several occasions—all when she was in her early twenties. This earned Ted Williams's lifelong respect and friendship.

- Struck out home run king Hank Aaron and other outstanding major league hitters.
- Her pitches were extremely fast—equivalent to a 119-mile-per-hour baseball, in terms of reaction time.
- When in California to attend Chapman College, Joan led the Orange Lionettes to the 1965 National Championship.
- Set an amazing LPGA (women's) and PGA (men's) record of just seventeen putts in one round of golf—a record that still stands over forty years later.
- Set a national tournament basketball single-game scoring record of sixty-seven points in 1964. Her basketball records were set long before the three-point shot was initiated.
- Played on the 1965 U.S. National Basketball Team.
- At age seventeen, set a National AAU Basketball record by scoring forty-four points in the Eastern Seaboard AAU Championship.
- Averaged thirty points per game (basketball).
- Four-time Women's Basketball Association (WBA) All-American.
- Three-time AAU Basketball All-American.
- Most Valuable Player in the 1956 Women's World basketball tournament at age sixteen.
- Founded the Connecticut Clippers "Power-Volleyball" team—a U.S. Volleyball Association (USVBA) team—and was the player-coach for the Connecticut Clippers.
- Named to the All-East U.S. Volleyball Association team.
- Won the bowling competition (181 average) in the ABC nationally televised *Superstars Competition*.
- Finished second in the tennis competition in the *Superstars Competition*. Also fared very well in the basketball, rowing, bike racing and swimming events against the greatest athletes in the United States at the time.
- Over one thousand victories as the women's head softball coach at Florida Atlantic University (FAU).
- Eleven conference championships at FAU.
- Eleven NCAA postseason tournaments.
- Eight-time College Coach of the Year while at FAU.
- Palm Beach County (Florida) Coach of the Year.
- First woman recipient of the prestigious Connecticut Sports Writers' Alliance's Gold Key Award and the first woman ever to be invited to the awards banquet on January 28, 1974. No

woman had ever broken the barrier in the organization's thirty-three years up until then.

- No. 2 ranked athlete in *Women's Sports National* magazine's Athlete of the Year (1976). Dorothy Hamill was ranked No. 1.
- No. 4 on *Hartford Courant*'s Best Athletes of the Century—highest female athlete chosen.
- No. 3 ranking of Athletes of the Millennium in Connecticut. Only woman in top three.
- Connecticut Athlete of the Year—first woman selected by the Connecticut Sports Writers Alliance.
- Lifetime Sport Achievement Award from National Girls and Women in Sports (NGWS).
- Joan Joyce Day was proclaimed on August 15, 2015, and on September 27, 2022, in Waterbury, Connecticut.
- A softball field was renamed Joan Joyce Field. The field is part of Municipal Stadium, where Joan struck out Ted Williams on several occasions.
- Joan Joyce softball league formed in Joan's honor. One of the very few athletes to have both a field and a league named after her.
- Joan Joyce golf tournament named in her honor.
- The Joan Joyce—Outstanding Pitcher Award is presented on an annual basis at the Women's Major Softball National Championship tournament to the outstanding pitcher in the WMS tournament.
- The *Joan Joyce!* musical was a hit play and performed to sold-out audiences at Stony Creek's Legacy Theatre. The musical will be performed in Joanie's hometown of Waterbury, Connecticut, in October 2023. The play is fabulous, and the belief is that this play will go much further after Waterbury.

PRAISE FOR JOAN JOYCE

Joan Joyce dominated the sport for twenty-six years. Her name is the biggest name in softball ever. But Joan was tops at everything—basketball, volleyball, bowling, cards, shooting pool, ping-pong—you name it, it didn't make any difference. She would always beat you!
—"Micki" Macchietto Stratton, Brakettes Hall of Famer

Left: Historic face-off between Ted Williams and the "teenage girl" Joan Joyce at Waterbury's Municipal Stadium. *Courtesy of Brakettes Photo Archive.*

Right: Joan Joyce famed slingshot windup. *Courtesy of Joan Chandler.*

Joan Joyce is the *legend in our great game of softball! She was an amazing athlete and an incredible coach.*
—*Michele Smith, ESPN analyst, two-time Olympic gold medalist*

Joan Joyce was a national treasure and a sports legend!
—*Margie Wright, St. Louis Hummers and NCAA coach*

Athletes like Joan Joyce come along only once in a lifetime. Babe Didrikson Zaharias certainly got all the credit from the media, but Joan, in my opinion, was even better! Joan knew no barriers. She has been a true pioneer of women's sports, a fantastic role model and an inspiration to so many young girls (and boys).
Joan Joyce was simply the best—period.
—*Jane Blalock, LPGA Tour player, LPGA Legends Hall of Fame and CEO, JBC Golf Inc.*

Athletic director/teacher Joan Joyce while at Waterbury's Mattatuck College. *Andrew Badinsky photography; courtesy of Janis Joyce.*

In my opinion, Joan Joyce was not only the greatest female softball player, but you can put her in the same class as elite male players such as Sandy Koufax and Mickey Mantle.
Joan Joyce was the greatest female athlete on earth!
—Carol Hutchins, hall of fame head softball coach of the University of Michigan

The story is all true. Joan Joyce was a tremendous pitcher, as talented as anyone who ever played. [responding to a newspaper account of his early 1960s matchups against Joan Joyce]
—*Ted Williams, hall of famer and Boston Red Sox great, December 30, 1999*

5

THE BRAKETTES

"The Greatest Dynasty in Women's Softball History"

From the very beginning, there was a commitment from the entire Brakettes organization dedicated to fostering a winning environment and to respecting the fundamentals of the game of softball on a daily basis—and always done with class. This winning organization from owner, managers, coaches, staff and players resulted in the creation of a dynasty and a culture of winning. This dynasty is simply known as the "Brakettes."
—Diane "Schuie" Schumacher, Brakettes

With a 91 percent winning percentage (4,471 games played, 4,058 wins, 413 losses), 40 national championships (ASA/WMS), 3 world championships, 23 National Hall of Fame members and 11 Olympians, the Brakettes are clearly the No. 1 name in women's fast-pitch softball history. Throughout the team's 76-year history, the Brakettes have remained synonymous with softball excellence and have been the barometer for measuring the success of women's softball.

The first Raybestos-sponsored women's team was formed in 1947. The team was known as the Raybestos Girls All-Stars and compiled a 16-4 record (the team lost by one run in the state quarterfinals). The tag All-Stars was dropped, and the team assumed the name Raybestos Brakettes, as the Stratford, Connecticut–based plant produced brake linings for automobiles and trucks. With an 18-2 mark, the Brakettes captured the Eastern Coast Women's Softball Championship. In 1950, the Brakettes won their first

Three legendary Brakettes pitchers: Donna Lopiano, Bertha Ragan Tickey and Joan Joyce. *Courtesy of Janice Nelson.*

national tournament game, edging the host Thompson team of San Antonio, Texas, 2-1.

The addition of Bertha Ragan solidified the Brakettes into not only a major contender but also a team that had the makings of a championship lineup.

The Raybestos Brakettes captured their first national softball championship in 1958. As noted, the Brakettes won the 1958 title by a score of 1–0. The team won the championship in dramatic fashion, based on the no-hit pitching of the teenage phenom Joan Joyce and the "storybook" inside-the-park home run in the final inning by Brakettes captain Mary Hartman. It was the beginning of an incredible forty national softball championship titles for the Brakettes team.

Recognized as the greatest organized women's sports franchise of all time, the Brakettes are unparalleled (forty championships!) and only approached by Major League Baseball's New York Yankees' twenty-seven World Series victories. The Raybestos Brakettes won eight straight titles from 1971 to 1978, a mark comparable to the Boston Celtics' domination in the 1960s or UCLA basketball from 1964 to 1973. As noted on the Brakettes website, the Brakettes organization is "The Greatest Dynasty in Women's Softball History."

Peggy Kellers and Brakettes team celebrate their championship. *Courtesy of Brakettes Photo Archive.*

Over four hundred players have proudly worn the Brakettes uniform. The Brakettes are widely known for their workmanlike character, professionalism and their total commitment to continuing the world's greatest softball tradition. All who have played for the Brakettes have made a significant contribution and are part of this wonderful legacy.

Former Brakette Amber Radomski summed up the Brakettes by saying "The Brakettes teams were a melting pot for the best players and the best people in the game. The Brakettes' successes on the field directly translate to their abilities to succeed in life".

It is safe to say that the Brakettes' "best of the best" is Waterbury's Joan Joyce, who is considered by many experts and fans to be the greatest female athlete of all time.

First Raybestos Girls Softball Team 1945

1947

L-R, top row- Manager Bernie Kaplan, Marge Wargo, Lorraine Meehan, Betty Smith, Joan Wallace, Tina Basso, Helen Yakubson, trainer Harold Schlachter
bottom row- Annette Verespy, Midge Milowski, Mary Primavera, Millie Elias, Kitty Oslensky, Fran Pruzinsky, Irene Keleshan

1956

L-R, top row- Kathy Ries, Mary Hartman, Joan Kammeyer, Joan Joyce, Ann DeLuca
middle row- Manager Bernie Kaplan, Joan Wallace, Bev Mulonet, Bertha Ragan, Micki Macchietto, Marie Heady
bottom row- Edna Fraser, Madeline Hartman, Mary Jane Hagan, Ann Gregorini, Marie "Jo-Jo" Ottaviano

1958

L-R, top row- Bertha Ragan, Barbara Abernethy, Joan Kammeyer Kincaid, Joan Joyce, Mary Hartman,
Joan Wallace, Brenda Reilly
middle row- Coach Al Martin, Micki Macchietto, Beverly Mulonet, Frances Spellman, Marie Ottaviano,
Beverly Connors, Manager Vin Cullen
bottom row- Sara Lou Beebe, Edna Fraser, Ann DeLuca, Louise Schippani

Above: Brakettes
teams: 1945, 1947,
1956 and 1958.
*Courtesy of Brakettes
Photo Archive.*

Right: Joan Joyce
representing Brakettes
International
Championship win.
*Courtesy of Brakettes
Photo Archive.*

Amateur Softball Association (ASA) National Championships

The Brakettes' twenty-eight ASA National Championships Titles were in 1958, 1959, 1960, 1963, 1966, 1967, 1968, 1971, 1972, 1973, 1974, 1975, 1976, 1977, 1978, 1980, 1982, 1983, 1985, 1988, 1990, 1991, 1992, 2002, 2003, 2004, 2006 and 2007.

Women's Major Softball (WMS) National Championships

The Brakettes' twelve WMS National Championships Titles were in 2010, 2011, 2012, 2013, 2014, 2015, 2016, 2018, 2019, 2020, 2021 and 2022.

World Championships

The Brakettes' three world championship titles were earned in 1974, 1978 and 1986.

National Softball Hall of Fame Inductions

Thus far, twenty-three Brakettes have been inducted into the National Hall of Fame. Rosemary "Micki" Stratton was the first Brakette inducted in 1969.

The Brakettes inducted are: Rosemary "Micki" Stratton (1969), Bertha Ragan Tickey (1972), Kathryn "Sis" King (1975), Pat Harrison (1976), Shirley Topley (1981), Donna Lopiano (1983), Joan Joyce (1983), Willie Roze (1985), E. Louise Albrecht (1985), Sharron Backus (1985), Peggy Kellers (1986), Rose Marie "Rosie" Adams (1987), Diane "Schuie" Schumacher (1992), Kathy Arendsen (1996), Gina Vecchione (1997), Barbara Reinalda (1999), Pat Dufficy (2005), Sheila Cornell (2006), Dot Richardson (2006), Allyson Rioux (2009), Lori Harrigan (2011), Lisa Fernandez (2013) and Sue Enquist (2015).

Non-players inducted into the National Softball Hall of Fame are William "Bill" Simpson, owner (1976); Vincent "Wee" Devitt, manager (1977); Joseph Barber, Connecticut ASA commissioner (1978); Ralph Raymond, manager (1993); and John Stratton (2023).

Brakettes program signed by all members of the Brakettes. *Courtesy of Brakettes Photo Archive.*

One of the all-time greatest softball pitching staffs, 1967. *Left to right*: Joan Joyce, Donna Hebert, Bertha Ragan Tickey, Donna Lopiano. *Courtesy of Jim Fetter.*

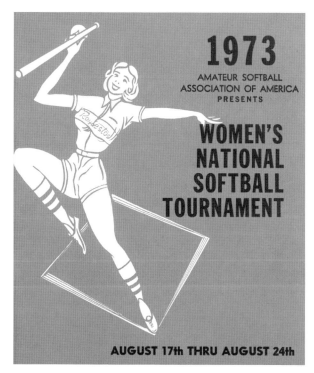

Left: A 1973 tournament program. *Author's collection.*

Below: Brakettes celebrate their national championship. Author's note: The bucket shown in the photo of the Brakettes celebrating the WMS championship was painted blue in honor of former teammate Danni Kemp, who passed away at the young age of nineteen. *Courtesy of Kathy Gage.*

Brakettes celebrate their 1992 championship. *Courtesy of Brakettes Photo Archive.*

Tatum Buckley's diving catch. *Courtesy of Kathy Gage.*

World Softball Hall of Fame

Brakettes Inducted into the World Softball Hall of Fame are Diane "Schuie" Schumacher (1993), Joan Joyce (1999), Kathy Arendsen (2003) and Sheila Cornell-Douty (2007).

Non-players inducted into the World Softball Hall of Fame are Ralph Raymond, manager (1993); Joseph Barber, Connecticut ASA commissioner (1999).

Brakettes Managers

- John Stratton (1995–present). In his twenty-seven years of managing the Brakettes, Stratton compiled a 1,450-138 record (95 percent), including 15 championships, two perfect seasons (63-0 in 2011 and 68-0 in 2013) and a 168-game winning streak (2010–12). John spent ten years at Florida Atlantic University (FAU) as pitching coach for FAU's head coach, hall of famer Joan Joyce.
- Ralph Raymond (1968–94). Ralph was a two-time Olympic team coach and was inducted into the National Softball Hall of Fame (1993).
- Vincent "Wee" Devitt (1962–67). Inducted into the National Hall of Fame (1977).
- Vin Cullen (1957–61). Led the Brakettes to their first national championship (1958).
- Bernie Kaplan (1947–56). Inducted into the Connecticut Softball Hall of Fame (1986).

Author's note: The following is a portion of an October 2, 2018 interview with current Brakettes manager John Stratton. In this interview, John discussed his upbringing in Stratford, Connecticut, and how he became involved in the Brakettes organization.

I hope readers find John's recollections of his early days interesting, informative and enjoyable.

TR John, where were you born and raised?

JS Right here in Stratford, Connecticut.

TR What schools did you attend?

John Stratton with hall of famer Joan Joyce. *Courtesy of Brakettes Photo Archive.*

JS   I graduated from Stratford High School. I then received my undergraduate degree in physical education from the University of Bridgeport (UB) and a master's degree from UB.

TR   Did you play any sports while in school?

JS   No, I had to work. I worked seven days a week, earning fifty cents an hour. I also mowed lawns and shoveled snow. So I was able to pay for my education with the money I earned. I would either take a bus to school or hitchhike. My parents didn't have the money to pay for school, so I had to earn the money. But I did play basketball and baseball in the summer because I was able to adjust my work schedule. I played baseball on the Lordship Little League team from 1947 to 1951 at the Raybestos Field. The league was sponsored by Raybestos. I went on to play baseball for the American Legion and Sterling House leagues. I pitched and played infield. I pitched for a lot of teams in the area. I even played a few games with the Raybestos Cardinals when they needed another player. They asked me to join the team, but I had to turn them down because I had to work and couldn't travel with the team. I also played a lot of basketball locally.

TR   How did you get involved with the Brakettes, and when did you become the manager of the Brakettes?

JS I was playing Little League ball, but I also followed men's fast-pitch softball at the time. The Raybestos Brakettes and the Raybestos Cardinals were just starting up. My dad asked me if I wanted to see the women's Brakettes team play. I was very curious since I had never seen a women's softball team. I was amazed at how good they were. At one point, the Brakettes team asked me to be their batboy. I said sure. I was nine years old. Actually, my main job was chasing foul balls because the officials really needed to get those softballs back [*laughter*]. So I did that for the women's team and the men's team. Every night after the game, my pay was one of the softballs. So I would get the softballs and throw them into a drawer. When I became seventeen years old, my mom said, "Hey, get these softballs out of the kitchen. I need the drawer space." I had collected two hundred softballs, so I decided to start my own team [*laughter*]. I learned how to pitch from the great Raybestos Cardinal Softball pitcher Johnny Spring. I used to pitch batting practice to the Brakettes players when I played for the Raybestos Cardinals.

JS Years later, I became a coach for the Brakettes in 1971. I managed the team on a temporary basis in 1976 and then permanently from 1995 to the present.

Other Notables in the Brakettes Organization

- Bob Baird | Brakettes general manager since 1988 and a Connecticut Softball Hall of Fame inductee (2017)
- Joe Barber | Brakettes longtime general manager. Barber was inducted into both the National and World Softball Hall of Fame.
- Kristine Botto Drust | John Stratton's assistant coach and former Brakette player. Inducted into the Connecticut Softball Hall of Fame (2018).
- John "Jay" Stratton | John Stratton's son, who coaches the Brakettes and has been involved with the team's staff since 2006. He is married to former Brakettes catcher Keri McCallum.

National Pro Fastpitch League (NPF)

The Brakettes joined the National Pro Fastpitch League in 2006 (while fielding an amateur team that won the national championship that year). The team reached the NPF Final, but the experiment only lasted that one season.

BRAKETTES HOME FIELDS

*"Softball Capital of the World" and the "Mecca of Women's Softball"
—two terms used by local media in reference to Stratford, Connecticut, and
the legendary Brakettes softball team.*

The Brakettes initially played their home games at Stratford's Raybestos
Memorial Field, named in honor of Raybestos employees who died in
World War II. For the 1974 World Championship, fifteen thousand fans
packed the park for the final game, which the Brakettes won, representing
the United States. It was the first world championship for the Brakettes,
who won nine games, all by shutouts. The field, which was located near the
Raybestos plant, closed at the end of the 1987 season.

The Brakettes have since played their home games at Frank DeLuca
Hall of Fame Field, named for hall of fame softball pitcher and Stratford
community icon Frank DeLuca.

Brakettes home game, early 1960s. *Courtesy of Brakettes Photo Archive.*

BRAKETTES PLAYERS

The Brakettes were comprised of athletes who have not only mastered their physical skills but they have also mastered the skill of being a great teammate. This combination proved to be the secret to winning
—Amber (Radomski) Morgan, Brakettes

Allyson Rioux, Second Base

- Hometown: Stamford, Connecticut
- Brakettes: 1979–88
- Games Played: 574
- Runs: 236
- Hits: 387
- Doubles: 51
- Inducted into the National Softball Hall of Fame: 2009
- Inducted into the Connecticut Softball Hall of Fame: 1989
- Sadly, Allyson passed away in 1987 at the tender age of twenty-seven.

Amber Radomski Morgan, Infield

- Hometown: Branford
- Brakettes: 2006–17
- Connecticut Softball Hall of Fame: 2017

Left to right: Allyson Rioux, Amber Radomski and Ann Deluca. *Courtesy of Brakettes Photo Archive and Kathy Gage.*

Ann DeLuca, Outfield

- Hometown: East Haven, Connecticut
- Brakettes: 1956–68
- Batting average in 1957: .327 (24 games)
- Connecticut Softball Hall of Fame: 1976

Andrea Duran, Third Base

- Brakettes: 2006 (NPF pro)
- Olympics: 2008

Barbara "Rusty" Abernethy, Pitcher

- Hometown: East Haven, Connecticut
- Brakettes: 1948–54, 1957–62
- Career pitching record: 145 wins, 40 losses
- Connecticut Softball Hall of Fame: 1980
- First director of women's athletics at Southern Connecticut State University

Barbara Reinalda, Pitcher

Barbara Reinalda was a steady, consistent, gamer—a real workhorse! She threw a heavy ball, didn't walk batters and played great defense as a pitcher.
—Diane "Schuie" Schumacher, Brakettes

- Hometown: Lakewood, California
- Brakettes: 1976–94
- Pitching record: 441 wins, 31 losses
- Games played: 675
- Hits: 282
- Doubles: 45
- Strikeouts: 2,172
- Holds record for least number of walks.
- National Softball Hall of Fame: 1999

Left to right: Andrea Duran, Rusty Abernethy and Barbara Reinalda (on the winner's podium, San Salvador, 1978). *Courtesy of Brakettes Photo Archive.*

Bertha Ragan Tickey, Pitcher

Everyone respected Bertha for her skills. She was kind of like a Lou Gehrig—a lot of class but not flash.
—Brenda Reilly, Raybestos Brakettes

- Hometown: Dinuba, California
- Brakettes: 1956–68
- Hits as a Brakette: 661
- Pitching: 757 wins and 88 losses (285-26 with the Brakettes)
- Strikeouts as a Brakette: 3,529
- Best Season Pitching Record as a Brakette: 1964 | 32-5 (0.23 ERA)
- 11 National Championships—4 with the Orange Lionettes and 7 with the Brakettes
- National Softball Hall of Fame: 1972
- Connecticut Softball Hall of Fame: 1973
- After retirement in 1968, Bertha became the executive director of Stratford's Barnum Festivals.

Beverly Mulonet, Shortstop

- Hometown: Wolcott
- Crosby High School 1956
- Brakettes: 1952–61, 1963–67
- World All-Star shortstop: 1958, 1959, 1961
- Career batting average: .283
- In 1959, Beverly finished second in batting average (.290) and led Brakettes in hits, RBIs, doubles and triples.
- Connecticut Softball Hall of Fame: 1980

Brandice Balschmiter, Pitcher

Brandice was a workhorse for the Brakettes during her twelve years with the team.
—brakettes.com

- Brakettes: 2006–8, 2010–18
- Career pitching record: 190 wins, 16 losses
- Strikeouts: 1,785
- Best single season pitching record: 36-2 (2012), ERA 0.76

BEVERLY MULONET — starts her ninth year with the Brakettes. The Waterbury native was selected for the second straight year as the World All Star Shortstop. She finished second in hitting with a .290 avg. She led the team in hits, RBI's, doubles and triples.

Left to right: Bertha Ragan, Bev Mulonet and Brandice Balschmiter. *Courtesy of Brakettes Photo Archive and Kathy Gage.*

Brenda Reilly, Utility Player

Brenda was our outstanding utility player for the Brakettes. She was one of few players at that level that could adapt to multiple infield positions with ease. She embraced everyone on the team with her sense of inclusion. Everyone mattered to Brenda. She was our team "cheerleader." Brenda always kept us entertained, usually at teammate Ann Deluca's expense.
—Pat Harrison, Brakettes

- Brakettes: 1956–66

Carol LaRose, Infielder

The Brakettes' "quiet" infielder. Carol wasn't flashy but she was "softball smart" and did her job at third base with precision and strength. She was like a wall, nothing got by her. Carol was a consummate team player who supported her teammates as they navigated the challenges of playing on a high-performance team.
—Pat Harrison, Brakettes

- Hometown: Bridgeport
- Brakettes: 1963–70
- Games Played: 485
- Runs: 258
- Hits: 445
- Doubles: 41
- RBIs: 200
- Connecticut Softball Hall of Fame: 1977

Catherine "Cat" Osterman, Pitcher

The astonishing accolades that Cat Osterman achieved during her playing career are among the highest in the game.
—Team USA Softball

- Brakettes: 2001–2, 2005
- Olympics: 2004, 2008, 2021

Left to right: Brenda Reilly, Carol Larose and Cat Osterman. *Courtesy of Brakettes Photo Archive and Bill Kurbs.*

Cecilia "Cec" Ponce, Outfield

- Brakettes: 1971–75
- Brakettes batting average: .280
- Earned first team All-Star honors in 1973

Cheri Kempf, Pitcher

- Brakettes: 1991–93, 1995
- VP of Athletics Unlimited
- Former president and commissioner of NPF softball league

Claire Beth "C.B." Tomasiewicz, Catcher

- Brakettes: 1973–75
- Batted .305 in 1974

Danielle Henderson, Pitcher

Danielle was a fierce competitor who had total command on the mound. A true Brakette. When batters faced Danielle, they really had to be on top of their game to have any kind of success off her.
—*Kristine Botto Drust, Brakettes assistant coach*

I would finish with my collegiate season then go straight into playing for the Brakettes. Coming together in the summer with your friends to play softball was some of the best summers I had. No matter how you played (good or bad), your teammates were always there to pick you up.

This taught me a valuable lesson in life—that even when things are not going well, there is always someone there to pick you up.
—Danielle Henderson

- Born and raised in Commack, New York
- Attended Commack High School and the University of Massachusetts
- Played basketball in high school
- Became a Brakette after playing against them with the LI Angels
- Brakettes: 1997–99, 2002–3, 2008
- Pitching record: 102 wins, 10 losses.
- Strikeouts: 1,357
- Helped the Brakettes end their decade-long championship drought in 2002
- Olympic gold medalist: 2000
- After the Olympics, she played in the NPF with the New England Riptide: 2005–6.
- Head coach of women's softball team at UMass

Danni Kemp, Utility Player

- Brakettes: 2015–16
- A very popular Brakette player
- Sadly, Danni passed away at the tender age of nineteen years old.

Denise Denis, Center Field

Included in many of the Brakettes all-time records, including home runs.
—brakettes.com

- Hometown: Trumbull
- Brakettes: 2005–19
- Games played: 738
- Runs: 743

- Hits: 857
- Doubles: 159 (Brakettes leader)
- Triples: 62
- Home runs: 135 (Brakettes leader)
- RBIs 713
- Batting champion: 2014 (.488)
- Connecticut Softball Hall of Fame: 2019

Left to right: Cheri Kempf (*third from left*) with Kelly Kretschman, Kellie Wilkerson, Stephanie Hill, Sarah Pauly, Danielle Henderson and Denise Denis. Note: This is the moment Denise set the all-time Brakettes home run record. *Courtesy of Brakettes Photo Archive and Kathy Gage.*

Diane "Schuie" Schumacher, First Base

Playing for the Brakettes was a life changing, ongoing opportunity. The Brakette players had the good fortune of being supported by an organization that was 100 percent committed to providing all the necessary resources, including financial support, needed to run an operation—fostering an environment to win and to win with class.
—Diane "Schuie" Schumacher

- Hometown: West Springfield, Massachusetts
- Brakettes: 1976–86
- Games played: 622
- Doubles: 97
- Triples: 48
- Home Runs: 23
- RBIs: 498
- Brakettes batting champion: 1976 (.382 BA), 1977 (.376 BA); 1978 (.356 BA); 1982 (.339 BA), 1984 (.356 BA)
- Pitching (11 games): 55 wins, 16 losses
- National Softball Hall of Fame: 1992
- World Softball Hall of Fame: 1993

Dionna Harris, Outfield

- Brakettes: 1990–94
- Hits: 325
- RBIs: 14
- Olympian: 1996

Donna Lopiano, Pitcher

No child should ever be told that they cannot pursue their dreams, both in sports and in life.
—Donna Lopiano

- Hometown: Stamford
- Brakettes: 1963–72

Clockwise from top left: Diane Schumacher, Dionna Harris and Donna Lopiano. *Courtesy of Brakettes Photo Archive.*

- Pitching record: 183-18 (winning percentage .910)
- Strikeouts: 1,633 and walked only 384 (817 innings, just under 2 per inning)
- Best single season pitching record (1972): 27-3 (ERA 0.14)
- Games played: 552
- As a batter: Hits: 518, Doubles: 65, Triples: 39, Home runs: 24, RBIs: 281
- Brakettes batting champion: 1970 (.316 average), 1972 (.367 average)
- All-American: 9 times
- MVP: 3 times (1966, 1971, 1972)
- National First Team All-Star 8 times
- National Softball Hall of Fame: 1983
- Connecticut Softball Hall of Fame: 1983
- Member of the Connecticut Clippers "Power-Volleyball" team
- Member of the Raybestos Basketball team
- Former CEO of the Women's Sports Foundation (1992–2007)
- Dr. Lopiano was named one of "The 10 Most Powerful Women in Sports" by Fox Sports.
- The Sporting News has repeatedly listed her as one of "The 100 Most Influential People in Sports."

Donna McLean, Outfield

Played the game at 100 percent unselfishly all the time from practice, to warm up, to the game. You never questioned her work ethic.
—Kristine Botto Drust, assistant coach

- Hometown: Torrington, Connecticut
- Brakettes: 1987–89, 1996–2005
- Games played: 656
- Batting: Runs: 284, Hits: 500, Doubles: 59, Triples: 31, Home runs: 19

Doreen "Doe" Denmon, Catcher

Doe was our main catcher for many years. She had the ability to successfully work with pitchers with a myriad of temperaments—difficult, easygoing, overconfident and those lacking in confidence. Doe was the only catcher I know of during that period of time to not wear typical catching shin guards. Instead she wore soccer shin guards under her white tube socks and volleyball knee pads. Doe took immense pride with her own game calling with no help from coaches, a rarity these days.
—Diane "Schuie" Schumacher, Brakettes

- Hometown: Stratford
- Brakettes: 1978–95
- Games played: 815
- Runs: 261
- Hits: 500
- Doubles: 75
- Triples: 30
- Home runs: 25
- RBIs: 275
- Connecticut Softball Hall of Fame: 2005

Dorothy "Dot" Richardson, Shortstop

I was just blessed to express the gifts God had given me.
—Dot Richardson

- Hometown: Orlando, Florida
- Brakettes: 1984–94
- As a 13-year-old, Dot began her fast-pitch softball career with the Orlando Rebels, where she played right field, third base.
- Games played: 542
- Runs scored: 431
- Hits: 644
- Doubles: 95
- Triples: 36
- Home runs: 22

Clockwise from top left: Donna McLean, Doreen Denmon and Dot Richardson (*sliding*). *Courtesy of Brakettes Photo Archive and Bill Kurbs.*

- RBIs: 225
- Brakettes batting champion: 1985 (.332), 1986 (.320)
- National Softball Hall of Fame: 2006
- Olympics gold medal: 1996, 2000

Edna Fraser, Outfield

Edna and Ann DeLuca were my outfield teammates when I joined the Brakettes in 1964. I was the new left fielder, Annie was in center and Edna was in right. They were my "outfield" mentors, ensuring that my experience was a success. Our communication was exceptional, thanks to their guidance.
—Pat Harrison, Brakettes

- Hometown: Milford
- Brakettes: 1953–64
- Brakette batting champion: 1954 (.357), 1976 (.340), shared with Joan Wallace and Jo-Jo Ottaviano
- Connecticut Softball Hall of Fame: 1975
- Head coach of Raybestos Robins farm team: 1965–74

Elaine Biercevicz (Piazza), Catcher

- Shelton High School ('64)
- High School Captain—Basketball team
- Colleges: SCSU, Springfield College
- Hamden, Connecticut resident
- Brakettes: 1966–70
- Connecticut Softball Hall of Fame: 2006
- Connecticut Women's Basketball Hall of Fame: 2012
- Lyman Hall High School (Wallingford) athletic director
- Elaine's mission has been to promote the important role that sports (especially softball and basketball) along with physical fitness play in the daily lives of young people.

Fran Sarullo, Infielder

- Brakettes: 1975
- Falcons: 1976–77

Gina Vecchione, Outfield

Some players deliver in clutch situations. Gina Vecchione was such a player during her 12-year career with the Raybestos Brakettes. More often than not, Gina delivered the game-winning hit or the go-ahead RBI to lead the Brakettes to another victory.
—National Softball Hall of Fame

- Hometown: New Rochelle, New York
- Brakettes: 1978–89
- Games played: 570
- Runs: 243
- Hits: 517
- Doubles: 72
- Triples: 38
- RBIs: 182
- Member of 6 national championship teams
- Solid defensive player with an accurate arm
- Batted .300 or higher 8 times, with a personal season best of .371 in 1982
- National Softball Hall of Fame: 1997

Ginny Walsh, Infielder

- Hometown: Milford, Massachusetts
- Brakettes: 1981–82

Irene Shea, Third Base

In the spring of 1973, a Buffalo teammate of mine introduced me to the legendary Joan Joyce at one of her volleyball matches. Later, the three of us played a round of golf, and Joan convinced me to try out for the Brakettes. I began my Brakette career as the leadoff hitter because of my speed and ability to also hit for power. My experience as a Brakette allowed me to establish a close relationship with many of my teammates, a relationship I will always treasure. There were many good times off the softball field as well, such as fun times on the golf course with Joan (she was a star in so many sports!), running mini camps for young girls and being involved in many motivational clinics with the Brakettes. The good times continued when I joined the Connecticut Falcons.

I loved playing the game of softball, and I knew I had the skills to play at the top level. Confidence plays such an important role in the game of softball!
—Irene Shea

- Hometown: Bainbridge, New York
- Education: BS (SUNY Brockport, 1966); master's in education (University of Buffalo, 1967); doctorate in education (University of Buffalo, 1971)
- Brakettes: 1973–75
- Runs: 201
- Hits: 305
- Triples: 32
- Brakettes batting champion: 1974 (.423 BA), 1975 (.421)
- Brakettes record: Most games played in a single season (86 in 1974)
- Brakettes record: Most hits in a single season (124 in 1974)
- Brakettes batting average: .395
- First team All-Star 1973–75
- National championship batting average: .545

Joan Joyce, Pitcher, First Base

I never worry about the batter, except to make sure the ball goes where I know it will do the most good. When I'm going right, there's nobody who can hit me.
—Joan Joyce

The following are some of Joan Joyce's statistics as a Brakette (only):

- Made Brakettes roster at age 13. Used mainly as infielder when she first joined.
- Brakettes: 1954–63, 1967–75
- Brakettes pitching record: 429-27
- Games played: 942
- Strikeouts: 5,677 (No. 1)

- Averaged nearly 2 strikeouts per inning
- Best single season pitching with Brakettes: 1974 (42-2, 0.17 ERA), 1973 (37-1, 0.08 ERA), 1975 (36-0, ERA 0.14), 1968 (35-3, 0.08 ERA), 1969 (30-6, 0.32 ERA), 1970 (27-1, 0.13 ERA). The 42 wins in 1974 is a Brakette record that may stand for years to come.
- Strikeouts in one season: 548 (1974), 491 (1968), 472 (1969), 463 (1962), 442 (1973), 415 (1961), 366 (1975), 349 (1963), 349 (1960), 331 (1970), 306 (1972)
- 76 strikeouts in 36 innings—a World Tournament record.
- Struck out 67 batters in a tripleheader (1961)— all in a single day
- As a Brakettes batter: overall batting average .327 (.406 in 1973); Hits: 940; Doubles: 153; Triples: 67; Home runs: 23; RBIs: 529
- Six-time Brakettes batting champion: 1960 (.394), 1962 (.303), 1967 (.365), 1968 (.343), 1969 (.325), 1973 (.406)
- National tournament batting champion in 1971, with a batting average of .467
- 18 straight years softball All-American
- Struck out every batter but 1 (who had walked) pitching a no-hitter against Australia in 1974 tournament
- Struck out all but 2 batters in a single game on at least 8 separate occasions
- 976 strikeouts in 36 innings (a world tournament record)
- Lowest earned run average in a world tournament (0.00)
- Most consecutive scoreless innings in a world tournament (36, a world tournament record)
- Most no-hitters in a world tournament (3, a world tournament record)

Left to right: Edna Fraser, Gina Vecchione and Joan Joyce. *Courtesy of Brakettes Photo Archive and Joan Chandler.*

- Most perfect games in a world tournament (2, a world tournament record)
- 4 straight no-hitters (1968)
- 70 scoreless innings in the 1974 ASA National tournament—in high-pressure games
- As a teenager: 2 no-hitters in her first 2 national tournament games (1958). A no-hitter (at age 17) in the quarterfinal game against Detroit, and 2 weeks after turning 18, she threw a no-hitter in the national championship game, walking only 1 batter while striking out 19.
- 2 no-hitter games in a national tournament—on 4 occasions
- 123 consecutive scoreless innings set in 1971 (set a Brakettes record)
- 229 scoreless innings in 1975 and a winning streak of 52 games
- Most shutouts in a season—38 shutouts—1974 (set a Brakettes record)
- 8-time MVP in the softball national tournament (set a Brakettes record). 1961, 1963, 1965 (with the Lionettes), 1968, 1971 (co-MVP), 1973, 1974 and 1975
- Most innings pitched in one game—29 in 1964—striking out 39 batters

Joanna Gail, Third Base

- Brakettes: 2007
- Olympics: 2004 (Greece)

Joyce Compton, First Base

- Brakettes: 1973–75
- RBIs: 142
- Triples: 28
- Hits: 84 in 1973, 1974
- Batting average: .338
- 1975: Led Brakettes in triples, doubles and RBIs
- 1975: Batted .429 in national tournament

Joanna Gail and Kaci Clark (*right*) with Brakettes Cat Osterman and Kaitlyn Flood. *Courtesy of Kathy Gage.*

Kaci Clark Zerbe, Pitcher

Kaci Clark was instrumental in the 2002 tournament and Championship Title. Kaci also played on the pro team in 2006.
—brakettes.com

- Brakettes: 2002–3, 2005, 2006 (NPF pro)
- 2002 pitching record: 29-0
- Strikeouts in 2002 national final: 12

Kaitlyn Flood, Catcher

- Brakettes: 2020–22
- Batting champion: 2021

Kathryn "Sis" King, Outfield

- Hailed from Cincinnati, Ohio
- Brakettes: 1965–67
- Brakettes batting average: .322
- 1965: Led Brakettes with a .352 batting average, 12 hits, including 4 triples

- 1959: First Brakette to hit a home run over the Raybestos Memorial scoreboard
- National Softball Hall of Fame: 1975

Kathy Arendsen, Pitcher

- Hometown: Zeeland, Michigan
- Growing up in Michigan, her idol was the legendary Joan Joyce of the Raybestos Brakettes.
- Pitched for the Holland Christian High School, where she pitched her team to the state championship.
- Kathy played basketball in her junior high and also high school, but her preference was softball.
- Education: Grand Valley State University, Texas Women's University (TWU) and Chico State University (CA). She pitched TWU and Chico to national championships.
- Kathy received the 1978 Broderick Award as the nation's outstanding female athlete in softball.
- Selected to pitch for Team USA at the 1979 and 1983 Pan American Games, winning a gold and silver medal, respectively.
- Brakettes: 1978–92
- Earned All-American honors 13 times; won 9 national championships; and 3 world championships
- In 1999, Kathy was ranked by *Sports Illustrated* as one of the 50 greatest sports figures from Michigan.
- Head coach at Mississippi State University, where she became the winningest coach in program history. Also, head coach at University of Oregon.
- Brakettes pitching record: 337-26 (0.15 ERA)
- Strikeouts: 4,061 (second to Joan Joyce)
- Brakettes record: 593 strikeouts in 1980
- Best single season records: 1981 (36-2, ERA 0.07), 1980 (34-3 ERA 0.07), 1982 (30-3 ERA 0.12)
- National Hall of Fame: 1996
- World Softball Hall of Fame: 2003

Left to right: Kathryn "Sis" King, Kathy Arendsen and Kathy Strahan. *Courtesy of Brakettes Photo Archive and Allan MacTaggart.*

Kathy Elliot (Krygier), Outfield

- Brakettes: 1974–1975
- Overall batting average: .387
- 1975: .388 BA
- 1975 National Tournament: .381 BA
- Possessed a strong throwing arm
- 1974–75: Second-team All-Star selection

Kathy Strahan, Shortstop

Playing softball was what I loved to do, so I decided to build a life with it.
—Kathy Strahan

Kathy Strahan was a very humble and unselfish player and person. She possessed soft hands when fielding and was soooo smooth, always making it look so easy. If I would give her a nickname it would be "smooth operator." She would throw perfect strikes to my glove at first base. "Stray" was a steady hitter for our Brakettes team.
—Diane "Schuie" Schumacher, Brakettes

- Hometown: Folsom, California
- Brakettes: 1977–81
- Became a successful softball coach at San Jose State under AD Irene Shea (former Brakette)

79

Kelly Kretschman, Center Field

- Brakettes: 2003, 2006 (NPF pro)
- Led the 2006 pro NPF team with a .410 batting average
- Olympics: 2004, 2008

Clockwise from top left: Kelly Kretschman, Keri McCallum (*with husband, Jay Stratton; Micki Stratton; John Stratton*), Assistant Coach Kristine Botto Drust (*with Brakettes manager John Stratton*). *Courtesy of Brakettes Photo Archive and Allan MacTaggart.*

Keri McCallum, Catcher

- Brakettes: 1998–2004, 2006
- Batting champion: 1998 (.391 BA)

Kristine Botto Drust, Outfield

- Hometown: Cheshire
- Brakettes: 2004
- Halls of fame inductions: Connecticut Softball Hall of Fame (2018), Lowell High School Hall of Fame and the UMass Lowell Hall of Fame
- New England Riptide (NPF) 2005–6 (member of the 2006 Riptide team, which beat the Brakettes for the NPF championship)
- Current Brakettes assistant coach: 2015 to the present

Author's note: For an interview with Kristine, please see Appendix B.

Lauren Pitney, Second Base

- Brakettes: 2017–20
- Batting champion: 2018 (BA .489), 2019 (BA .524)
- Home runs: 30
- RBIs: 142
- Head coach of the Select Brakettes Team: 2021, 2022

Linda Finelli, Right Field

When you played for the Raybestos Brakettes, it was made clear to every player that you always stood for the flag and you were never to disrespect that uniform and what it represents. We all were grateful for the opportunity to be a part of the Brakette organization.
—Linda Finelli

- Hometown: Waterbury, Connecticut
- Brakettes: 1971–74

Left to right: Lauren Pitney, Linda Finelli and Lisa Fernandez. *Courtesy of Brakettes Photo Archive and Kathy Gage.*

- Raybestos Robins: 1967
- Linda's rookie year, Brakettes had an undefeated season at 57-0

Lisa Dennis, Outfield

- Hometown: Stratford
- Bunnell High School
- Brakettes: 1976–77
- Connecticut Softball Hall of Fame: 2020

Lisa Fernandez, Pitcher, Third Base

- Hometown: Long Beach, California
- Brakettes: 1990–94
- Pitching record: 60-3
- 1997: MVP, outstanding pitcher (USA national championship)
- 1998: USOC Top 10 Athlete of the Year Award
- Olympic gold medalist: 1996, 2000, 2004
- National Softball Hall of Fame: 2013

Lori Harrigan (Mack), Pitcher

- Hails from Las Vegas, Nevada
- Brakettes: 1993–94
- Olympic gold medalist: 1996, 2000, 2004
- National Softball Hall of Fame: 2011

Lucille "Lu" Gecewicz, Outfield

- Brakettes: 1974–75
- Brakettes career: .339 BA
- 1975: .352 BA, 31 RBIs, 8 triples
- Speedy outfielder
- Accurate throwing arm
- Raybestos Robins: 1969–70

Marie "JoJo" Ottaviano, Infield

- Brakettes: 1951–63
- Batting champion: 1953 (.339 BA), 1956 (.340 BA, shared with Joan Wallace and Edna Fraser)

Left to right: Lori Harrigan, Marie Ottaviano and Mary Hartman. *Courtesy of Brakettes Photo Archive and Bill Kurbs.*

Mary Hartman, Outfield

- Hometown: New London
- Batting Champion: 1957 (.388 BA)
- Hit historic home run in the 1-0 1958 championship game (Brakettes' first championship)
- Hit 8 home runs in 1958
- Batting champion: 1957 (.388 BA)
- Brakettes captain: 1958, 1959

Mary Primavera, Pitcher

- Hometown: Albany, New York
- Stratford High School graduate
- Brakettes: 1947–52
- Connecticut Softball Hall of Fame: 1986
- 19-year-old Primavera was a Broadway singer at the same time she was playing for the Brakettes.

Nikki Myers, Pitcher, Utility Player

- Hails from St. Petersburg, Florida
- Brakettes: 2002, 2006 (NPF pro)
- Brakettes Pitching (2002): 15-0, 0.08 ERA, 164 strikeouts
- Brakettes Batting Champion (2002): .416 BA
- Florida Atlantic University: two-time All-American and three-time All-Sun Conference Player of the Year
- Michigan State University: Assistant Coach

Pat "Duff" Dufficy, Utility Player

"Duff" has some of the best offensive numbers in Brakettes history and played more Brakettes games than anyone.
—brakettes.com

- Hometown: Trumbull
- Brakettes: 1977–83, 1985–95, 1997

Clockwise from top left: Pat Dufficy, Mary Primavera and Nikki Myers. *Courtesy of Brakettes Photo Archive and Kathy Gage.*

- Games played: 1,112 (all-time Brakettes leader)
- Runs: 788 (all-time Brakettes leader)
- Hits: 1,177 (all-time Brakettes leader)
- Doubles: 148
- Triples: 80 (all-time Brakettes leader)
- Home runs: 91
- RBIs: 752 (all-time Brakettes leader)
- Brakettes batting champion: 1992 (.423)
- National Softball Hall of Fame: 2005

Pat Harrison, Outfield

My teammates were an awesome group of dedicated, elite athletes who represented the best our sport had to offer. They loved the game and were so proud of their achievements as Brakettes. I was now in for the ride of my young career—no one could have been more in love with being able to say, "I am a Brakette."
—Pat Harrison

- Hometown: Vancouver, British Columbia, Canada
- Brakettes: 1964–72
- Games played: 482
- Hits: 430
- RBIs: 189
- National First Team All-Star 3 times
- Brakettes batting champion: 1966 (.301), 1971 (.340)
- National Softball Hall of Fame: 1976

Pat Whitman, Pitcher

- Brakettes: 1974–75
- 1974 pitching record: 38-3, ERA 0.45 (second best single season pitching record in Brakettes history, behind Joan Joyce)
- Career pitching record: 69-6

Clockwise from top left: Pat Harrison, Peggy Kellers and Elaine Biercevicz (Piazza), Pat Whitman. *Courtesy of Brakettes Photo Archive.*

Peggy Kellers, Catcher

Our teammates focused on the motto, "When you're a champion you have to work harder than anyone else."
—Peggy Kellers

- Hometown: Stratford
- Brakettes: 1964–74
- Games played: 529
- Runs: 196
- Hits: 289
- All-American 6 times
- National Softball Hall of Fame: 1986
- Connecticut Softball Hall of Fame: 1982
- Head softball coach at University of Virginia

Rachele Fico, Pitcher

Rachele has the most wins in an undefeated season (33 in 2010) by any Brakette not named Joan Joyce.
—Brakettes.com

- Brakettes: 2008–12
- Career pitching record: 94-1

Rose Marie "Rosie" Adams, Second Base

The "Energizer Bunny." Rosie's quick hands and feet at second base were a pleasure to watch. Her quick movements turned double plays into works of art! She was full of life both on and off the field.
—Pat Harrison, Brakettes

- Hometown: Escondido, Californiia
- Brakettes: 1971–74
- First Team All-American: 1971–73
- Played in WPS league for Santa Ana (1976) and Buffalo Breskis/Bisons (1978)

- Served in the U.S. Navy for 12½ years, retiring as a lieutenant commander
- National Softball Hall of Fame: 1987

Rosemary "Micki" Macchietto Stratton, Catcher

Micki was a great catcher, a terrific hitter and a great teammate. She was a great "slapper" and bunter. Micki was the first Brakette to be inducted into the National Softball Hall of Fame, which says a lot. More importantly, Micki was a wonderful person and my best friend.
—John Stratton, Brakettes manager and husband of Micki Stratton

- Hometown: Stratford
- Brakettes: 1956–65
- Games Played: 481
- Runs: 297
- Hits: 488
- Triples: 22
- RBIs: 140
- Brakettes batting champion: 1959, 1961, 1965
- National Softball Hall of Fame: 1969 (first Brakette inducted)
- Connecticut Softball Hall of Fame: 1972

Left to right: Rachele Fico, Micki Stratton during 1962 national tournament and Sarah Pauly. *Courtesy of Brakettes Photo Archive and Kathy Gage.*

Sarah Pauly, Pitcher

A tall, strong, dominant pitcher.
—Kristine Botto Drust, Brakettes assistant coach

- Brakettes: 2005, 2006 (NPF pro)

Sharron Backus, Shortstop

Offensively and defensively, Sharron was always a threat. She was a clutch player who made tough plays look easy. You could always feel that she was present in every moment of every game or practice. She worked hard at being an All-Star shortstop.
—Pat Harrison, Brakettes

- Hometown: Anaheim, California
- Brakettes: 1969–75
- National Softball Hall of Fame: 1985

Sheila Cornell (Douty), First Base

- Hometown: Phelan, California
- Brakettes: 1988–94
- Runs: 290
- Hits: 462
- Doubles: 77
- Triples: 48
- Home runs: 44
- RBIs: 393
- Batting champion: 1988 (.436), 1989 (.440), 1990 (.432), 1993 (.450)
- National Softball Hall of Fame: 2006
- World Softball Hall of Fame: 2007
- Olympian: 1996, 2000

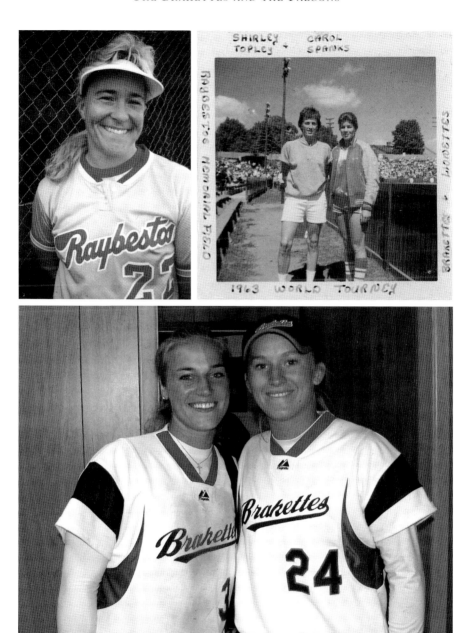

Clockwise from top left: Sheila Cornell Douty, Shirley Topley (with Carol Spanks, Lionettes) and Stephanie Best (with Jessica Merchant). *Courtesy of Brakettes Photo Archive and Kathy Gage.*

Shirley Topley, First Base

Canada's international softball legend! One of the most powerful players and coaches in Canadian and U.S. softball history. Instrumental in guiding and promoting the softball careers of many young women, including myself at age fifteen. I will be forever grateful that she was and is still part of my life.
—Pat Harrison, Brakettes

- Hometown: Hondo, Alberta, Canada
- Brakettes: 1963–64
- Batting champion: 1963 (.372), 1964 (.340)
- National Hall of Fame: 1981
- Olympian assistant coach: 2000
- Raybestos Robins coach: 1963–64

Stephanie Best, Infielder

- Brakettes: 2004, 2006 (pro)
- Batting champion: 2004 (.367)

Stephanie "Steffi" Call, First Base, Pitcher

Holds Brakettes record for the longest home run ball with a 344 foot home run (over the men's stadium center field fence).
—brakettes.com

- Brakettes: 2011–14
- Game played: 202
- Runs: 217
- Doubles: 44
- Home runs: 79 (1 out of every 7 at bats). Steffi holds 3 of the top 4 home run records for a single season in Brakettes team history, including a record 31 in 2011.
- RBIs: 263
- Batting champion: 2013 (.533 BA)
- Single season pitching record: 2013 (27-0, ERA 0.42)
- A member of the Florida Atlantic University softball team

Sue Enquist, Center Field

Susie had a gun for an arm out in center field. She would throw runners out at home with that arm on a perfect bounce. She could bunt on a dime and would slide head first to bases successfully without injury, which Coach Raymond was not a big fan of. Susie was a natural pied piper as other players would follow her all over the place.
—Diane "Schuie" Schumacher, Brakettes

Sue Enquist was perhaps the most intense teammate I ever played with, in any sport or on any team. One of the first things I found out about Sue was she played to win, and nothing was going to stop her.
—Kathy Strahan, Brakettes

- Hometown: San Clemente, California
- Brakettes: 1976–81
- National Softball Hall of Fame (Meritorious Service): 2015

A flying Enquist

Clockwise from top left: Steffi Call with Joan Joyce, Sue Enquist, Val Suto and Tatum Buckley's diving catch. *Courtesy of Brakettes Photo Archive and Kathy Gage.*

Sue Tomko, Infield

- Brakettes: 1971–74

Tatum Buckley, Second Base

Tatum was a true "gamer." The word I would use in watching her all-out effort on the softball field is "Wow!"
–Kristine Botto Drust, Brakettes assistant coach

Known for her fine defensive play, especially diving catches in the infield.
—brakettes.com

- Brakettes: 2014–17
- Outstanding defensive infielder

Valerie Suto, Center Field

A Brakette through and through. Our leadoff batter and a true batting champion
—Kristine Botto Drust, Brakettes assistant coach

- Brakettes: 2015–21
- Batting champion: 2015 (BA .465), 2016 (BA .530)

Willie Roze, Second Base

- Hometown: Hamden
- Brakettes: 1966–75
- Games played: 629
- Runs: 359
- Hits: 526
- Doubles: 66
- Triples: 29
- RBIs: 203
- National Softball Hall of Fame: 1985

Several Opponent Players

Carol Spanks, Orange Lionettes, Shortstop, Third Base

Carol Spanks was the toughest player for me to get out. She had a good batting eye. In my opinion, she was one of the best hitters in the game. I actually developed a special screwball pitch just for her (down and in) to get her out.
—*Joan Joyce, Brakettes, Falcons*

At California Polytechnic Institute, Carol established a reputation as the coach who was able to get the full potential out of her athletes. They believed they could beat anyone and often did.
—*Sue Enquist, Brakettes*

- Buena Park Kittens: 1951–53
- Buena Park Lynx: 1953–57
- Orange Lionettes: 1958–75
- ASA All-American: First team (10 times), second team (3 times)
- Starred in 4 national championships: 1962, 1965, 1969, 1970

Carol Spanks. *Courtesy of Brakettes Photo Archive.*

- Led the league in hitting: 1954 (.328), 1969 (.400), 1970 (.321), 1971 (.327), 1972 (.400)
- Batted over .400 in 4 national championships: 1967 (.438), 1972 (.417), 1973 (.429), 1975 (.545)
- Lionettes batting average: .322 BA (700 hits in 2,176 at bats)
- Outstanding defensive player award in national championships: 1968, 1969, 1970
- Pitching: 122-28 (ERA 0.72)
- Head coach at California Polytechnic Institute (15 years)
- Associate head coach at UNLV (5 years)
- NFCA Hall of Fame (as coach): 1994
- National Hall of Fame: 1981

Charlotte Graham, San Jose Sunbirds Pitcher

- Santa Clara Laurels: 1968–75
- Pitched for 4 different WPS pro teams: 1976–79
- Posted a 23-11 pitching record (ERA 0.93) for the San Jose Sunbirds: 1976. Led the Sunbirds to a World Series berth, losing to the Connecticut Falcons.
- 1977: Led the Santa Ana Lionettes to a World Series berth, losing to the Connecticut Falcons.
- 1978: Pitched for the Buffalo Bisons
- 1979: Pitched for the New York Golden Apples
- Charlotte's "go-to pitch" was her rise ball.

Dot Wilkinson, Phoenix Ramblers Catcher

- Hometown: Phoenix
- National Softball Hall of Fame: 1970
- Arizona Sports Hall of Fame: 2020
- Member of the Phoenix Ramblers: 1933–65, national softball champions 1940, 1948 and 1949
- Batting averages with the Ramblers: .455 (1954), .450 (1955), .387 (1957).
- Dot was also a terrific bowler and was inducted into the International Bowling Hall of Fame (1990)

Margie Wright, St. Louis Hummers Pitcher

- St. Louis Hummers of Women's Professional Softball League: 1977–79
- Pitching record with St Louis Hummers, 1978: 20-11
- Margie pitched Game 2 of the 1978 WPS World Series against the Connecticut Falcons
- 1979: Pitched Game 4 of the 1979 WPS World Series against the Falcons
- Margie was the head softball coach at Fresno State from 1986 to 2012 and led the team to the NCAA National Championship in 1998.
- Ranks second all-time in career victories among NCAA Division 1 coaches.
- Inducted into the National Fastpitch Coaches Association Hall of Fame: 2000
- Inducted into the International Women's Sports Hall of Fame: 2001

Mary Lou Pennington, San Jose Sunbirds Catcher

One of the smartest catchers in the league.
—Laura Malesh, Brakettes

Author note: The following is a portion of an interview I conducted with Mary Lou Pennington

TR How did you get involved in sports?

MP I was involved in sports ever since I was a little kid. I can remember when I was in elementary school, I couldn't wait to go out and play softball with the other kids. I have three sisters and two brothers, and we would play a lot of sports three on three. That's what we did when we were kids, whether it was softball or some other sport. We played a lot of softball in our backyard. Because I was not allowed to play Little League baseball, I joined a Bobby Sox softball league when I was fourteen years old.

TR How did you decide to become a catcher?

MP It was out of necessity. When I was fifteen years old, I played third base for the Rio Linda Pixies. But the team needed a catcher and asked me if I

Mary Lou Pennington. *Courtesy of Mary Lou Pennington.*

could handle the position. I told them I could. Once I got back there, that was it. I continued to be a catcher on all the teams I played with.

TR When did you begin playing women's fast-pitch softball?

MP I became involved with women's fast-pitch in 1966 playing for the Rio Linda Pixies. I also played for the Roseville Lassies in 1970.

TR When did you play for the Santa Clara Laurels?

MP I played for the Santa Clara Laurels in 1974.

TR Did you play in the Women's Professional Softball (WPS) league? If so, what teams did you play for?

MP In 1976, I played for the San Jose Sunbirds. The Sunbirds won the Western Division Playoff series by sweeping the Santa Ana Lionettes in three straight games. This enabled us to play against the Connecticut Falcons in the WPS Championship. We had a good team and played the Falcons tough, but the Falcons prevailed and won the 1976 WPS title.

TR Who did you play for in the 1977 season?

MP In 1977, I played for the Santa Ana Lionettes, along with Charlotte Graham, Donna Lopiano and Jackie Ledbetter. We won the Western Division playoff series 3 games to 1, earning the right to play the Connecticut Falcons for the 1977 WPS championship. However, the Falcons once again won the championship title that year.

TR Did you play for any other teams in the WPS league?

MP Yes, I played for the New York Golden Apples in 1979, the final season of the WPS league. Charlotte Graham was my teammate on this team.

TR Did you catch for Charlotte Graham? If so, what was her "go-to" pitch in critical situations?

MP Yes, I was pretty much Charlotte's exclusive catcher. She was a great pitcher and a great competitor. Charlotte was a speed pitcher. Her "go-to" pitch was the rise ball.

TR When did you first play against the Brakettes? Did you bat against Joan Joyce?

MP I first played against the Brakettes when I was with the Roseville Lassies. What I remember from that game is that Joan Joyce hit me on the wrist with one of her pitches and sent me to the doctor. I think I got a taste of Joan Joyce's incredible rise ball [*laughter*]. Thought I broke my wrist. I was in complete and total awe of Joan. I consider Joan Joyce the greatest pitcher of our generation. If you put Joan Joyce on any team, that team would win the championship. She was that good! Whatever team Joan played on, that team won.

TR What are your memories of playing with the teams you were on?

MP I enjoyed playing on all the teams I was on and all of my teammates. I love team sports. I enjoyed every minute of fast-pitch softball.

6

THE WOMEN'S PROFESSIONAL SOFTBALL LEAGUE (WPS)

The Women's Professional Softball League is the first women's professional league and the first to be owned by women athletes. I guess we're pioneers. We're working to pave the way for girls and women in years to come.
—Billie Jean King, tennis great and co-founder of the WPS

The Women's Professional Softball League (WPS, aka IWPS) was formed in 1976. The co-founders of WPS were tennis star Billie Jean King, pitching icon Joan Joyce and sports entrepreneur Dennis Murphy. The formation of the league was announced by Billie Jean at a press conference on April 6, 1976, in Meriden, Connecticut.

As stated in the WPS 1976 pamphlet:

> *The WPS is the first opportunity for women to perform as professionals on a team basis, the first chance to reap the rewards professional male athletes have enjoyed since Babe Ruth made [baseball] our national pastime. Women's Professional Softball stands at the forefront of that new coming generation. If we may steal a line from the Virginia Slims: "You really have come a long way, Baby!"*

The 1976 pamphlet further states that the formation of the WPS league aims to "revolutionize the concept of sports for women, offering women equality as athletes."

The WPS began as a two-division league consisting of ten teams. The Eastern League consisted of the Connecticut Falcons, the Buffalo Breskis

Billie Jean King and Joan Joyce announcing the Connecticut Falcons team. *Courtesy of Joan Chandler.*

(Bisons), the Chicago Ravens, the Michigan Travelers and the Pennsylvania Liberties. The Western League consisted of the San Diego Sandpipers, the San Jose Sunbirds (Rainbow), the Santa Ana Lionettes, the Southern California Gems and the Arizona Bird. Several other teams joined the league in the following years, including the Bakersfield Aggies, the St. Louis Hummers, the Edmonton Snowbirds and the New York Golden Apples.

Each team played a 120-game schedule (60 home and 60 away games), including 60 doubleheaders. The season lasted from May until September, concluding with championship playoffs and the World Series. The first WPS games were played on May 28, 1976: Michigan versus Southern California, Pennsylvania versus Chicago; Santa Ana versus Connecticut and San Jose versus Connecticut. The first All-Star game was played on July 28, 1976, in Michigan.

SUMMARY OF THE WPS

The WPS league was made up of many powerhouse teams from around the country. The league existed for four years from 1976 to 1979, at which time the league was forced to close due to lack of funds.

Clockwise from top left: Joan Joyce proudly displays the 1976 championship banner and Joan at podium after the Falcons won the first Women's Professional Championship in 1976; a jubilant Sandy Fischer (*pitcher*) celebrates after posting the last out of the 1978 WPS World Series; and Falcons celebrate the WPS Championship. *Courtesy of Joan Chandler.*

The Connecticut Falcons won the WPS Championship all four years. The Falcons WPS World Series victories were against the San Jose Sunbirds in 1976, the Santa Ana Lionettes in 1977 and the St. Louis Hummers in 1978 and 1979.

WPS MVP Awards for all four years were as follows:

1976   Joan Joyce (39-2, 494 strikeouts)
1977   Joan Joyce (24-4)
1978   Joan Joyce (18-1) and Donna Terry (15-2)
1979   Joan Joyce (20-6)

7

THE CONNECTICUT FALCONS

Our strong points are pitching, hitting, and fielding.
Our strength is that we have very few weaknesses—and we win.
—Irene Shea, Connecticut Falcons, 1976–79

The Connecticut Falcons played in the Women's Professional Softball League. The co-owners of the Falcons were tennis titan Billie Jean King, softball star Joan Joyce and golfing great Jane Blalock.

Jane reminisced about meeting Joan Joyce and her involvement in the Falcons organization.

I first met Joan Joyce at the 1975 ABC-TV Superstars Competition. What I discovered immediately was her wonderful personality, her sense of humor and her very unassuming nature. I saw someone who was totally down to earth—humble and normal. Joan was a very charismatic person and someone you just wanted to be around. We instantly became friends for life.

I was in total awe of the career that Joan Joyce had on the softball field. You can just see the frustration on the batters' faces after trying to hit a softball that must have looked like a blur to them, and the ball moved so dramatically!

Billie Jean King had announced that she was about to form a women's professional softball league together with Joan and Dennis Murphy. I became aware of the fact that Joan and Billie Jean were interested in

Connecticut Falcons jubilant after their championship. *Courtesy of Joan Chandler.*

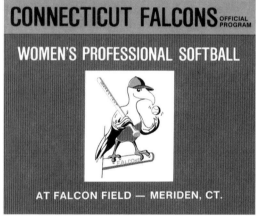

Above: Very first Connecticut Falcons tryout, 1976. *Courtesy of Mary Lou Pennington.*

Left: Connecticut Falcons logo. *Author's collection.*

forming the Connecticut Falcons which would play in the WPS. Knowing that the Falcons would be composed of many outstanding players from the legendary Brakettes, I jumped at the opportunity to become a co-owner of the Connecticut Falcons.

Without question, the Connecticut Falcons were the dominant team of the WPS, winning the championship title all four years of the league's existence (1976–79).

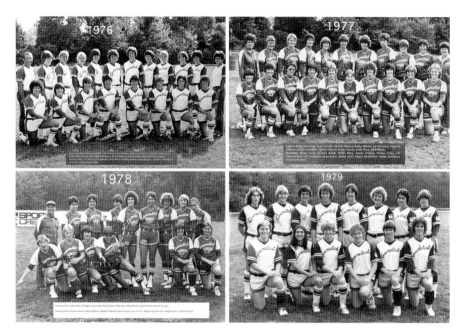

Falcons teams, 1976–79. *Courtesy of Joan Chandler.*

Falcons players celebrate their championship. *Courtesy of Joan Chandler.*

Falcons' outstanding clutch hitter Joyce Compton. *Courtesy of Joan Chandler.*

FALCONS PLAYERS

Annette Fortune, Outfield

- Hometown: Granville, Massachusetts
- Education: BA and master's degree (physical education) at Appalachian State University (ASU) in Boone, North Carolina. At ASU, Annette starred in women's softball and hockey.
- Falcons: 1976–79
- Versatile all-around athlete, with outstanding speed and base running skill
- Taught at East Granby High School in Connecticut
- University of Hartford women's softball coach

Audrey "Audi" Kujala, Outfield

A speedy and adept outfielder, as evidenced by her .967 fielding percentage in 1978. In the 1977 WPS World Series, "Audi" was Connecticut's top slugger with a .500 batting average.
—IWPS website

- Hometown: Camden, New Jersey
- Falcons: 1977–79
- Acquired by Falcons in 1977 draft
- A speedy and adept outfielder
- 1978 fielding percentage: .967

Cecilia "Cec" Ponce, Outfield

Considered by many to be a "clutch" performer, in that she consistently hits in key spots and comes up with big plays in the field.
—IWPS website

- Hometown: Placentia, California
- Falcons: 1976
- Clutch hitter
- Possessed fine defensive skills and a strong throwing arm

Claire Beth "C.B." Tomasiewicz, Catcher

A fine defensive catcher and one of the key factors in the success of the Falcons' pitching staff. "C.B." was also a clutch hitter for the Falcons.
—IWPS website

- Hometown: Weston
- Falcons: 1976–77
- 1977: .283 batting average
- One of the Falcons' premier clutch hitters

Top to bottom: Annette Fortune, Audi Kujala and Cec Ponce. *Courtesy of Joan Chandler.*

Left to right: C.B. Tomasiewicz, Donna Terry and Fran Sarullo, 1976. *Courtesy of Brakettes Photo Archive, Joan Chandler and Kathy Gage.*

Donna Terry, Pitcher

Donna was another player greatly influenced by Joan Joyce. She realized she wanted to be a softball pitcher when, as a young athlete, she was in awe of Joan Joyce's pitching ability when Joan pitched for the Orange Lionettes at the National Tournament in Orlando. A fine pitcher, Donna was also an excellent pure hitter.
—IWPS website

- Hometown: San Juan, Puerto Rico, but moved to Florida
- Falcons: 1976–78
- 1976: second for the Connecticut Falcons in the batting average department with a .328.
- 1976–77: Owns a two-year .302 batting average with the Falcons
- 1977: 13-7 record and 3.00 ERA; added a win in the World Series, tossing a five-hitter win over Santa Ana, as well as a save
- An excellent pure hitter

Fran Sarullo, Infielder

- Falcons: 1976–77
- 1976: 15 RBIs in only 120 plate appearances
- Former Brakettes infielder

Ginny Walsh, Utility Infielder

Ginny was mainly utilized by the Falcons as a utility infielder. A fine defensive player with a strong throwing arm.
—*IWPS website*

- Hometown: Milford, Massachusetts
- Falcons: 1979
- Her versatility was an asset to the club, able to play shortstop, second and outfield
- Very good defensive player with a good throwing arm

Irene Shea, Third Base

Irene was one of the Falcons' most consistent hitters and ranked among the league leaders as a defensive third baseman. She supplied a lot of punch at the plate and was a sparkplug as a defensive infielder.
—*IWPS website*

- Hometown: Banbridge, New York
- Falcons: 1976–77
- Batting average 1976–77: .327 BA
- Impressive .958 fielding average
- Struck out only three times in 1976

Jackie Ledbetter, Catcher

When I played for my high school team (Granite Hills High), we had a pitcher that nobody could catch. I was a left-handed shortstop at that time. The coach asked if I would try catching, and I said sure. So, from that day on I was a catcher.
—*Jackie Ledbetter*

- Education: Lemon Grove Elementary (Lemon Grove, California), Granite Hill High School (El Cajon), Sacramento's Cal State University (physical education major)
- 1977: southpaw catcher, right fielder for Santa Ana Lionettes

Top to bottom: Ginny Walsh, Irene Shea and Jackie Ledbetter (in China, 1979). *Courtesy of Joan Chandler.*

- Batted .308 against the Falcons in the 1977 World Series (4 hits in 13 at bats)
- 1978–79: catcher for Connecticut Falcons
- Batted respectable .265 (18 RBIs) in 1978
- Assistant women's softball coach at the University of California at Berkeley

Joan Joyce, Pitcher, First Base, Co-Owner of the Connecticut Falcons

Joan Joyce is the real deal, a fierce competitor and one of the greatest athletes and coaches in sports history. She is a champion in sports and in life.
—Billie Jean King, sports icon and co-founder of the WPS

Author's note: For a list of other sports accomplishments by Joan Joyce, please refer to the previous chapter on Joan Joyce and also the Brakettes chapter.

- Co-founder of the Women's Professional Softball League (WPS)
- Player, coach, co-owner of the Connecticut Falcons professional softball team
- Behind Joan's brilliant pitching, Connecticut Falcons won the championship in all 4 years of the league's existence
- Because of Joan's dominance as a pitcher, the league invoked the "Joan Joyce Rule," which moved the pitcher's mound back by four feet. The purpose was to hopefully cause her to be more in line with the other pitchers in the league. Despite this rule, Joan continued to be the most dominant pitcher in the WPS.
- Joan Joyce was named Most Valuable Player (MVP) for all four years of the Women's Professional Softball League (1976–79).

Joyce Compton, First Base

An outstanding defensive first baseman, "J.C." was also a torrid at the plate and one of the best clutch hitters in the game.
—IWPS website

- Born in Trenton and raised in Robbinsville, New Jersey.
- Education: Windsor Elementary School (Windsor, New Jersey), Sharon Elementary School (Robbinsville, New Jersey), Allentown High School (Allentown, New Jersey); graduated in 1972 from Trenton State College (Ewing, New Jersey)
- Falcons: 1976–79
- 1977: .283 regular season batting average (76 hits) and led Falcons in hits (76) and home runs (7) and RBIs
- 1977 WPS Championship: .429 batting average
- 1978: Posted a lofty .355 batting average (regular season) and .300 BA (1978 World Championship)
- 1978: Led team last summer in at bats (287), hits (102), doubles (26), triples (7), total bases (172), runs batted in (57) and fielding percentage (.990)
- All-Pro first baseman
- Mattatuck Community College (Waterbury, Connecticut) athletic director and coach of softball, volleyball and basketball teams. Joyce Compton replaced Joan Joyce as coach at Mattatuck.

Clockwise from top left: Joyce Compton, Joan Joyce's look of determination and Judy Martino. *Courtesy of Joan Chandler.*

- Head coach at the University of South Carolina from 1987 to 2010
- National Softball Hall of Fame: 1983
- World Softball Hall of Fame: 1999
- Connecticut Softball Hall of Fame: 1983

Judy Martino, Catcher

Judy is one of those players who played several positions well and was called on for utility duty throughout the season. Outside of being a fine catcher, Judy played the outfield as well as second and third base.
—IWPS website

- Very versatile player for the Falcons
- In her career, Judy participated in the national tournament 10 times and made all-regional honors 7 times.
- Played for Falcons in 1976

Karen Gallagher, Shortstop

- Hails from Chicago
- Falcons: 1977–79
- 1978: .284 BA (14 extra-base hits 26 RBIs)
- 1978: only 12 strikeouts in 261 at bats
- 1978: Played in 86 of the Falcons' 88 regular-season games

Kathy Elliot (Krygier), Outfield

Aside from being one of the top hitters in the lineup, Kathy has one of the finest throwing arms in the WPS league. One of the rules around the league is "Don't challenge the throwing arm of Kathy."
—IWPS website

- Falcons: 1976
- As a Brakette: .387 batting average (1974–75)

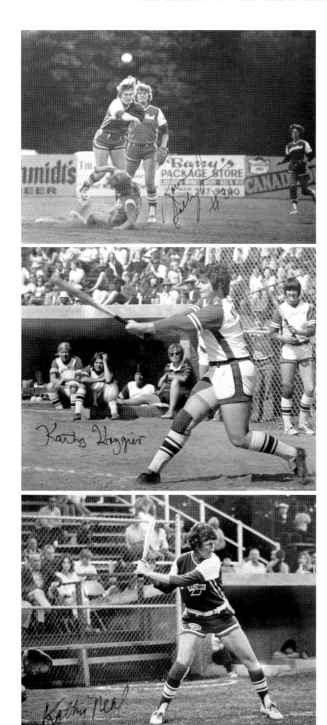

Top to bottom: Karen Gallagher, Kathy Elliot Krygier and Kathy Neal. *Courtesy of Joan Chandler.*

Kathy Neal, Pitcher

A fire-balling right hand pitcher, Kathy was the Falcons' number one pick in the WPS league draft. Aside from her pitching ability, Kathy was able to handle other positions during her softball career, such as outfield and first base.
—IWPS website

- Hails from California
- Falcons: 1976–78
- Falcons No. 1 pick in WPS draft
- 1976: No. 2 pitcher for the Falcons, compiling an impressive record of 19-10 and a 1.09 ERA
- 1976–77: Batting average .267
- Was the East's starting pitcher in the 1976 All-Star game

Kathy Stilwell, Outfield

Kathy was a fine all-around athlete, enjoying the sports of softball, volleyball, tennis, and basketball. A versatile player for the Falcons, Kathy played shortstop, second base and the outfield. Kathy was the Falcons' top hitter in 1977 with a sparkling .352 batting average.
—IWPS website

- Hometown: Garnett, Kansas
- Falcons: 1977–79
- 1976: .269 BA
- 1977: Falcons' top hitter with .352 BA and led Falcons in hits (76), doubles (17) and triples (9)
- Led WPS in triples and was second in the league in batting and doubles
- Versatile: Played shortstop, second base and outfield
- 1978: .289 BA and led Falcons in runs scored (64), stolen bases (13) and walks (44)

Left to right: Kathy Stilwell, Linda McMorran and Lu Gecewicz. *Courtesy of Joan Chandler.*

Linda McMorran, Shortstop

Another fan favorite, Linda compiled a sparkling .307 batting average with 11 home runs and 54 RBIs in her initial season with the Falcons in 1978. Also starred defensively at third base, registering a .943 fielding percentage.
—IWPS website

- Falcons: 1978–79
- 1978: .307 batting average with 11 home runs and 54 RBIs in her initial season with the Falcons in 1978
- Also starred defensively at third base (and sometimes shortstop, with a .943 fielding percentage)
- Main hobby: Surfing

Lucille "Lu" Gecewicz, Outfield

"Lu" Gecewicz was one of the Falcons' best all-around players and one of the fastest outfielders in the WPS league. One of the league's premier defensive outfielders, "Lu" made only six errors in two seasons with the Falcons. She possessed a strong, accurate throwing arm and was also a solid hitter. Lucille had a loyal following at Falcon home games.
—IWPS website

- Hometown: Middletown
- Falcons: 1976–78
- Raybestos Robins: 1969–70

Margaret Rebenar, Pitcher

Known for her blazing fastball and good all-around batting.
—IWPS website

- Hometown: Phoenix
- 1978: 11-5 record (1.77 ERA)
- Known for her blazing fastball

Rayla Jo Allison, Catcher

- Hometown: Fort Worth, Texas
- Falcons: 1977–79
- Versatile: Mainly used as catcher, but also played infield and outfield and pitched
- 1978: .289 BA with 11 RBIs and only struck out 8 times in 121 at bats
- 1978: .980 fielding percentage

Sandra "Sandi" Hamm, Third Base

In addition to fast-pitch softball, Sandra involved herself in a variety of sports including: volleyball, hockey, basketball, and skiing.
—IWPS website

- Hometown: Terryville
- Falcons: 1976
- Member of: U.S. Volleyball Association (1969–71), AAU Basketball team (1970), U.S. Eastern Amateur Ski Association (1968–70) in Stratton, Vermont

Sandy Fischer, Pitcher

Sandy came to the Falcons in a three-team, four-player trade at the beginning of the 1976 season. Pitched with good velocity and a baffling change-up.
—IWPS website

Clockwise from top left: Sandra Hamm, Rayla Jo Allison and Margaret Rebenar. *Courtesy of Joan Chandler.*

- Hometown: Quincy, Illinois
- Falcons: 1976–79
- 1977: Despite a 7-8 won-lost mark, Sandy posted a respectable 2.78 ERA, second lowest on the team and eighth best in the league. Allowed only 47 hits and 20 walks, striking out 27 in 97 innings of work
- 1978: 12-6 won-lost record (1.44 ERA), with 43 strikeouts
- 1976–79: posted a victory in all four World Series

Clockwise from top left: Sandy Fischer, Sharron Backus and Snooki Mulder. *Courtesy of Brakettes Photo Archive and Joan Chandler.*

Sharron Backus, Shortstop

Sharron is best known for her excellent fielding and her throwing arm which was very apparent to those who saw her play. A clutch hitter.
—IWPS website

- Hometown: Anaheim, California
- Falcons batting average: .264
- Selected to the Eastern All-Star squad as an All-Pro Shortstop

Snooki Mulder, Outfield

Snooki was a premiere defensive outfielder. She possessed excellent speed, a strong throwing arm, and good control of the bat. Snooki makes things happen when she gets on base.
—IWPS website

- Hometown: Eustis, Florida
- Falcons: 1976–79
- A 3-team, 4-player trade prior to the 1976 season brought Snooki to the Falcons.
- 1977: Led Falcons with 16 sacrifice hits and 14 stolen bases, ranking second and fourth, respectively, in the league in those categories.
- Excellent control of the bat
- 1978: Owned a .954 fielding percentage previous summer
- Hobby: motorcycles

Sue Tomko, Infielder

Sue was a valuable asset to the Falcons team. Along with her solid hitting, Sue was a fine defensive player at several infield positions with the Falcons.
—IWPS website

- Hometown: Wallingford
- Falcons: 1976
- Known for her defensive ability, solid hitting and versatility.

Sue Tomko (*left*) and Willie Roze (*sliding*). *Courtesy of Joan Chandler.*

- Was an outstanding basketball player at New Haven's Southern Connecticut State College, which ranked third in the United States during Sue's four varsity seasons.
- Aside from softball, Sue was also involved in basketball, volleyball and field hockey.

Willie Roze, Second Base

One of the league's most versatile players. A slick-fielding second baseman, Willie also possessed outstanding base-running ability. Her speed keyed many runs for the team. Willie was also a solid batter for the Falcons.
—IWPS website

- Hometown: Hamden
- Education: BA and master's degree from New Haven's Southern Connecticut State College
- Falcons: 1976–79
- 1976: .285 batting average, 7 home runs and selected All-Pro infielder
- Has the distinction of hitting the first home run in WPS history in the Falcons' 1976 season opener against Buffalo
- 1977: The Falcons' fourth-leading hitter with a .296 batting average, collecting 68 hits, including 16 extra base hits.

- 1977: Posted a .928 fielding percentage, led the Falcons in scoring 43 runs
- 1977: Batted .357 in World Series with 5 hits in 14 at bats
- 1978: batted .286 with five home runs and 29 RBIs, including a double and triple along with a .300 offensive effort in the World Series
- A perennial All-Star for the Falcons.
- One of softball's most versatile players, Willie's most valuable asset was her speed, a sparkplug who keyed many rallies.

8

FALCONS IN CHINA

I was told we were the first U.S. team to play in mainland China. So we were a novelty to the Chinese people, who probably never saw Americans before. We were treated super well by everyone.

I vividly remember the massive crowds that would attend our games. When we did our clinics with them they had so many questions, wanting to learn more about softball from us. When Joan Joyce gave a clinic, they would actually bring out measuring sticks to measure where her foot would land after throwing the ball. They had cameras on Joanie everywhere and filmed all of her pitching deliveries They were so in-tuned in wanting all the knowledge that they could get from us. When we sat down for dinner, they would bring out a dictionary of sports terms and have us explain what certain sports expressions meant such as "taking the collar" or "choke." We would have to explain these terms to them, which was fun. Probably my favorite thing was visiting the Great Wall. Phenomenal. We actually played catch at the Great Wall.

—Joyce Compton

In May 1979, the general manager of the Connecticut Falcons (John Salerno) arranged for the Falcons to visit China on a historic fourteen-day, six-game goodwill tour. The fifteen-member Falcons were the first professional U.S. athletic team ever invited to compete on the mainland. The team's motto was "To China with Glove."

The Connecticut Falcons arrive. *Courtesy of Joan Chandler.*

Bottom Row (left to right) – Margaret, Joyce, Kathy N., Willie, Donna, Sandy, and Joan
Top Row – Rayona, Karen, Kathy S., Snooki, Rayla, Andi, Brenda, Linda, Annette and Jackie

Playing softball on the Great Wall

This page, top to bottom: Falcons in China, 1979; Joan Joyce "freezes" rival batter during the Falcons' China tour (most bats didn't leave the batters' shoulders); and Falcons playing softball at China's Great Wall. *Courtesy of Joan Chandler.*

Opposite: Joan the Pied Piper. People flocked around Joan Joyce throughout the *entire* China goodwill tour. *Courtesy of Joan Chandler.*

While in China, the Falcons competed in softball games, conducted softball clinics and even played friendly games of basketball against Chinese players.

All six softball contests were won by the Falcons, but the games were fairly close. The games were played in Beijing and Lanzhou, China.

The Connecticut Falcons played their final game in China on Friday, May 25, 1979. In this game, Joan Joyce pitched a no-hitter, barely missing a perfect game (with only one walk) in front of an overflow crowd in Lanzhou, China, of forty-five thousand fans.

9

"TOO STRENUOUS"?

Women Banned from Baseball

Girls are not allowed to play in baseball.
—former MLB Commissioners

In 1931, Baseball Commissioner Kenesaw Mountain Landis banned female players from professional baseball. His theory was that baseball was "too strenuous" for women. The ban was subsequently upheld several times, including a 1952 ruling by MLB Commissioner Ford Frick. The result of these bans prevented talented women, especially fast-pitch players, from competing in MLB's minors or major leagues. Thus, women turned to softball as a means of recreation.

It is a fallacy to believe that members of teams like the Brakettes who participated in the Amateur Softball Association were not tough both mentally and physically, just because they played softball as opposed to baseball. Nothing could be further from the truth. Game after game these players proved that they were more than up to the task of withstanding the physical and mental rigors associated with playing fast-pitch softball on a high level.

Consider the fact that catchers on women's fast-pitch softball teams at the time did not wear shin guards or foot guards. They did wear knee pads but otherwise no real protection. Significant injuries were bound to occur and did. Take, for instance, catching against a pitcher like Joan Joyce. A closely monitored study of her pitches revealed that she threw a softball equivalent to a 119-mile-per-hour baseball in terms of reaction time. Pitches at that speed would sometimes have a devastating effect not only on the batter but

Top: Ball heading toward Brakette player's head; *bottom*: nice block of home by Falcons C.B. *Courtesy of Joan Chandler.*

also on the catcher. Joyce's drop ball moved dramatically and was extremely devasting. As Joan recalled, "Up until the mid-seventies, catchers wore knee pads but no shin or foot guards. We lost a catcher for the entire year when a foul tip from a drop ball broke her foot."

For a very long time, women softball batters never wore batting helmets or batting gloves. In addition, they all wore shorts, metal cleats and no sliding

This page, top: Tough headfirst slide; *bottom left*: tough stretch by both players; *right*: collision at first. *Courtesy of Joan Chandler.*

Opposite, top: *Clockwise from top left*: Falcons Joyce Compton sliding home; Brakettes Micki and "The Big Out"; very hard slide by NY Apples Dawn Forster. *Courtesy of Brakettes Photo Archive and Joan Chandler.*

Opposite, bottom: Kathy Stilwell's daredevil leap to second base. *Courtesy of Joan Chandler.*

pads. Abrasions, bruises and cuts were commonplace. Players were known to dive headfirst into second base or crash into a catcher in an attempt to reach home—just as their male counterparts were doing in baseball's MLB.

"Too strenuous"? The photos in this chapter disprove that theory!

10

FUN

When I look back on my athletic career, one word comes to mind—Fun. I mean, how many people can say they have gone through their entire life having fun in what they were doing? I'll let all my accomplishments speak for themselves. But to me, I loved every sport I was involved in and whether it was as a player, a referee or a coach it has all been fun.
—Joan Joyce, 2018

As previously noted, the Brakettes are the most successful women's softball team in history. They produced some of the most talented female athletes of any sport. Their records and achievements speak for themselves. And the same is true for the highly successful Connecticut Falcons teams.

Take, for instance, the legendary softball players Joan Joyce and Bertha Ragan Tickey. When you watched them pitch (as I did, watching Joan pitch for her teams), you had the feeling that you were in the company of greatness. And you were. For many, the terms *perfection* or *near-perfect* easily come to mind. And they were right.

Following the Brakettes and the Falcons dynasties and watching the precision, confidence and unbeatable attitude that all the players on these two teams played with, you had the feeling that winning was in their DNA. You almost felt that they were some kind of mechanical "robots." Well, that's not exactly true because what people didn't see was all the hard work, dedication and sometimes the overwhelming odds in reaching the championship that these women learned to deal with day after day.

Near-perfection would be an appropriate term—but only as it pertains to the players on these two teams when they were *on* the field. *Off* the field was another story, indeed. They were not robots, not in the least. They were just regular everyday people like you and me. And add to that the stress of having to work full time to make ends meet because the Brakettes were never paid for work as players and the Falcons were paid, but at a minimum level. I can speak with some degree of expertise since Joan Joyce became a very dear friend of mine. She would tell me some amazing stories of her experiences with the Brakettes and Falcons. I asked her one time if she would share her salary figure while she was with the Falcons. Joanie responded, "Sure, my salary was $1.00 per year."

But they knew how to have fun and not to take their sport too seriously. As Amber (Radomski) Morgan of the Brakettes explained, "The most amazing aspect of competing with the Brakettes was the players' abilities to turn on the fun in the dugout while moments later being able to intently focus on the field. This essentially allowed for the athletes to maintain a relaxed intensity that ultimately contributed to raising their level of play."

The players on both the Brakettes and Falcons teams truly played for the love of the game.

Clockwise from top left: Falcons clowning before game, Cathy Irvine of Buffalo Breskis/Bisons and Brakettes checking their gold medals. *Courtesy of Kathy Gage and Joan Chandler.*

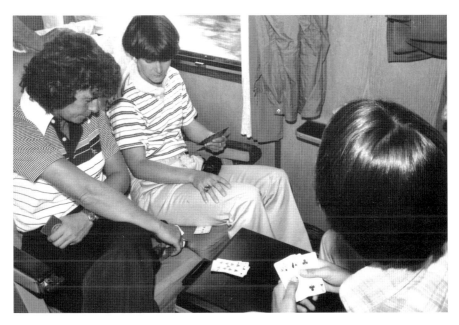

"Joanie was tops in everything. Heck, you wouldn't want to play cards or ping pong with her—she was so competitive, and she would always win!" John Stratton, Brakettes manager. *Courtesy of Joan Chandler.*

Brakettes manager John Stratton gets doused with a bucket of ice after the Brakettes won the 2004 National Championship. *Courtesy of Allan MacTaggart.*

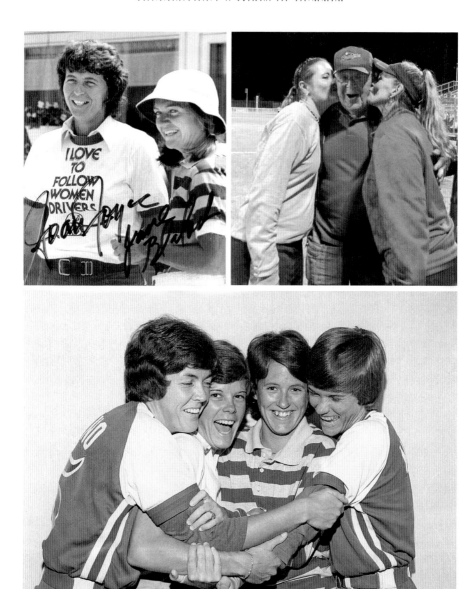

Clockwise from top left: Joan Joyce and Jane Blalock share a laugh during an LPGA tournament; Ellen "Frankie" Spruce, John Stratton and Donna McLean; members of the Falcons celebrating their championship win. *Courtesy of Brakettes Photo Archive and Joan Chandler.*

Above: Mandie Fishback laughs hysterically as home run star (but slow runner) Steffi Call finally reaches home plate. *Courtesy of Brakettes Photo Archive.*

Right, clockwise from top left: Falcons clowning around before game; Brakettes' Jessica Mouse and Ashley Waters goofing around; Joan Joyce and Jane Blalock clowning around during the ABC-TV *Superstars* competition. *Courtesy of Kathy Gage and Joan Chandler.*

Joan Joyce and Snooki Mulder sharing a laugh at China's Great Wall during the Falcons Goodwill Tour. *Courtesy of Joan Chandler.*

Falcons clowning around dancing before game. *Courtesy of Mary Lou Pennington.*

Right: Brakettes Jessica Mouse and Ashley Waters clowning around. *Courtesy of Kathy Gage.*

Below: Brakettes in a relaxed, fun moment before the game. *Left to right*: Diane "Schuie" Schumacher, Dottie Richardson and Allyson Rioux. *Courtesy of Schuie Schumacher.*

11

RECOLLECTIONS

What Softball Means to Me

Author's note: I asked some former fast-pitch softball players, coaches and non-players to share their recollections of their playing days and, in the case of non-players, observations of teams and players they were associated with. I also asked them to share their thoughts on what softball means to them and the important role that softball has played in the lives of young girls and women. I believe you will find their responses enlightening.

Here are their responses:

AMBER (RADOMSKI) MORGAN, BRAKETTES

The ultimate dream come true

Lacing up your cleats to step onto the diamond with some of the most talented players in the game is both an incredible honor and a truly humbling experience. There are so many amazing players who wore the Brakettes uniform, and to be part of such a legendary tradition is truly exhilarating.

Getting called up to the Brakettes organization was the ultimate dream come true. The Brakettes were a melting pot for the best players and the best people in the game—all great ball players with the right attitude, including some players who had the opportunity to participate in the Olympics. (It wasn't until 1996 that women's fast-pitch softball was included in the Olympics.)

The sport of softball is a microcosm of life. All fast-pitch softball players are dealt a series of obstacles they must try to overcome if they hope to be successful in this sport. Just as in life, failure is bound to occur over the course of a season. And just as in life, the most important thing is to learn how to deal with these obstacles. The more you learn how to deal and overcome these setbacks, the more successful you will be, both in the game of softball and in the game of life.

Throughout their illustrious history, the Brakettes were successful because they worked extremely hard to embrace these adversarial conditions with grace, dignity and a little humor. They have always been taught the great balance and understanding of striving to be their personal best while at the same time mastering the skill of being a great teammate. The legacy of the Brakettes teams is their ability to succeed at a very high level and thrive in this sport as true competitors, as champions, and with the common goal of always putting the team first. This combination proved to be the secret to winning.

For many players, things just seem to fall into place, those who genuinely want their teammates to succeed, and who appear to have mastered, through hard work, what many others consider to be pure luck.

A teammate shares the same uniform, the same water jug and may even share the same bat and helmet. Great teammates share the same goal, while accepting their role and remaining prepared at every moment, and they form a lasting bond. This concept evolves as players mature and recognize that their contributions will change on a daily basis. However, the common goal always remains the same.

Doubleheaders and tournament play can be exhausting for the fans and the umpires—but for players it's all they know. Great memories are made when everyone catches tournament fever.

Brakettes fans are lifelong. I know this because I was one. Many of the faces never change; they may get a few more wrinkles from enduring the bright summer sun at the ballpark, but their loyalty remains the same. They are a constant sea of red and the best independent evaluators in the stadium, who are never afraid to share their thoughts and perspectives with the umpires. As softball players, we appreciate their cheers and of course the truth in our errors. They have been students of the game longer than many of the players have been alive.

When playing at the highest level, your opponents play a critical part in your success. Great teams continue to rise above when challenged. And the Brakettes teams, over the years, have been challenged by the best in the game.

Many members of the Brakettes have discovered that because of their success on the softball field, they have been able to further their careers in the field of coaching, teaching and advocating for women in sports.

This is the important lesson I have learned, having played at a very high level in fast-pitch softball.

BEVERLY "BEV" MULONET, BRAKETTES

An experience I will never forget and one that I will always cherish.

I remember one particular play that Jo-Jo Ottavanio and I always got a kick out of talking about. On this particular play, Jo-Jo played third base and I was at shortstop.

With a runner on second, a hard-hit ball narrowly missed Jo-Jo's diving attempt, but I managed to backhand the ball. The baserunner on second immediately ran to third once she saw that Jo-Jo could not reach the ball. I was about to throw the ball to Jo-Jo who was covering the third base bag, when I noticed that Jo-Jo had already put the tag on the girl sliding into third. To our amazement—and delight—the umpire called the girl out at third. But the ball was still in my glove! Jo-Jo and I just looked at each other and then ran very quickly and gleefully into the dugout, since that was the third "out." Once we got into the dugout, we all laughed our heads off. No one was going to tell the umpire that he was wrong!

When I was fifteen years old, I traveled with my team to Orange, California, to play in a national tournament hosted by the Orange Lionettes. Before leaving California, each of us purchased a bag of delicious oranges to bring home to Connecticut. I remember seeing a photo of four of us sitting on a bench relaxing when someone took our picture. Mary Hartman was still holding her precious cargo of oranges that she didn't want to part with.

Playing on the Brakettes team was an experience I will never forget and one that I will always cherish. The Brakettes owner, Bill Simpson, was so generous and supportive to every member of the Brakettes team. He paid for many of our road trips that we took after winning important games. At first, we would travel in cars that were loaned to us by the Raybestos

Bev Mulonet (*standing*), Mary Hartman (*holding her "precious cargo"*), Barbara Abernathy and Ann DeLuca. *Courtesy of Brakettes Photo Archive.*

organization. Either the coaches or some of our players with driver's licenses would drive the car. (I was too young.) Raybestos then purchased a bus that we used for our travels to games or for road trips.

I loved and respected all of my very talented teammates, admired all of our opponents, and of course, our fans were the absolute best!

CAROL HUTCHINS

When I played for the Lansing Laurels, it was a thrill of a lifetime when the Brakettes came to Lansing, Michigan, to play against our softball team.

I was absolutely starstruck the first time I saw Joan Joyce. It wasn't until Joan came on the scene that I really had a female role model who inspired me to play team sports. She is the reason why I got into softball.

Batting against Joan Joyce was terrifying! Batters would go up there and just hope to make some sort of contact. The first time I got to bat against Joan, I fouled one off, and we all thought it was cause for celebration!

It was such an honor playing against all the outstanding Brakette athletes and a very memorable experience!

DANIELLE HENDERSON, BRAKETTES

My teammates were always there to pick me up when needed.

Being a Brakette was an incredible experience. The historic significance and the successful history behind the Brakettes organization make you proud to be a part of it.

We must always remember the important role played by the very talented softball pioneers that have enabled young girls (women) to dream of one day becoming a member of a softball team and perhaps becoming a softball star themselves. We, indeed, stand on the shoulders of these pioneers who made it possible for players such as myself to achieve a level of success that was unimaginable in their day. Some of us have even had the incredible experience of becoming an Olympian—an opportunity these pioneers never had since they were not only banned from baseball but also banned from participating in the Olympics.

Coming together in the summer with friends to play the game of softball was some of the best summers I had. You can always be assured that no matter how you played the game, your teammates were always there to pick you up. And that was so important to me and my teammates. We played a lot of games all summer long in preparation for the nationals. We had some of the best times at national tournaments.

I remember that we would be put up in a house for the summer, and there were about ten of us that lived there. The Fairfield house I got to live in was close to the beach. (I believe college students lived there during the school year.) There were enough people in the house that you would always be able to find somebody that wanted to go to the movies, shop at the mall, go to the beach, pay a visit to a nearby town or find some other fun activities. I am from Long Island and worked at UMass so I would be able to go home or back to work during the week.

Although the Brakettes were technically an amateur team, the intensity with which the team has played throughout the years was comparable to major league baseball —the big difference, of course, is that the Brakettes never received ANY renumeration for their hard work. They truly played for the love of the game!

Softball is a fast-paced game compared to baseball. The viewership that softball has drawn over the years, especially with college softball, is remarkable. The Women's College World Series shows how much people enjoy watching these games. College play has some of the highest ratings on ESPN, and this year there was a game on ABC. Being played at a fast pace, you get to see the players hustle and make defensive plays as good as any MLB player. And you see them actually having fun! While softball players are very competitive, they know the importance of good sportsmanship and always cheer their teammates on despite the score.

Fast-pitch softball is such a great sport for all of these reasons, and I have enjoyed playing it at all levels. It is why I am a college softball coach. I want to give back to the sport that has given me so much in life.

DENISE DENIS, BRAKETTES

At one point, Danni Kemp had a major issue with her eyesight (double vision). It so happened that I had a migraine at one of our games. We were joking about our mutual issue with not being able to see well. When Danni got up to bat, I would say "swing" or "no" as the ball came out of the pitcher's hand. When she hit the ball, I remember jumping for joy so high because I thought it was a home run, but still I was so happy for her when the ball hit the fence. We had a good laugh when Danni came back to the dugout.

Later at a homerun derby, Danni began kidding me as I got up to the plate with Barbara Reinalda pitching. Despite the fact that Danni was battling the tumor at this point, Danni yelled out to me, "You better hit a home run—after all, I almost hit one and I couldn't even see the ball!"

Sadly, Danni's health issue turned out to be DIPG brain tumor. We lost her at the very young age of nineteen. Danni and I were extremely close, and I miss

Danni Kemp and Denise Denis after Danni's near home run. *Courtesy of Brakettes Photo Archive.*

her very much. The entire team loved Danni, and we all think of her all the time.

There is a support group on Facebook in Danni's honor called the Danni Kemp Cancer Support Group.

DIANE "SCHUIE" SCHUMACHER, BRAKETTES

A life-changing ongoing opportunity that resulted in a commitment from the entire Raybestos Brakette organization dedicated to fostering a winning environment, respecting the fundamentals of the game of softball on a daily basis and always done with class!

In 1976, Barbara Clark wore Donna Lopiano's uniform, and I wore Joan Joyce's uniform. We felt there were intangible forces propelling us to win our first ASA National Championship. This was especially important to us since the championship was being played at Stratford's Memorial Field, the stadium where Joan and Donna had attained such incredible successes.

Our Brakettes team played against the heavily favored Sun City Saints for the nationals. Their entire team remained intact while the entire Brakette team went to the newly formed pro WPS league—with the exception of Barbara Clark and Beth Quesnel. And so, when we won the title both Barb and I finally felt we earned the right to be a Brakette.

Maybe wearing those uniforms of those two legendary players helped—who knows?

Barbara Reinalda was my first roommate in a house in Milford. We didn't cook great meals. In fact, when making spaghetti for the players staying there, while dumping the water out of the large pan, we dumped the entire spaghetti into the sink. No worries, we just put the spaghetti back, rinsed it and served. No complaints.

Another roommate of mine in Milford was Sue Enquist. Susie was a dedicated surfer from California who never really acclimated herself to the hot, humid weather in Connecticut.

Susie loved to chew flower seeds. I called them bird seeds. She called me Big Bird. She could spit those things across the room, accurately hitting me. I called her Little Bird. She loved to be mischievous in a playful way.

Our Brakettes team had the wonderful experience of outstanding coaching from the late legendary manager Ralph Raymond, third base coach John Stratton and the late first base coach Andy Van Etten. Just as important, we played and practiced with teammates who were truly dedicated to winning on a daily basis, who were devoted to excellence and who always set their sights on becoming national champions.

I remember that during nationals our manager Ralph Raymond would insist that our team stay at a different hotel to keep us away from our competitors. I always thought this was a smart move. We avoided any interaction or distraction, especially when teams would lose. We would only have a curfew if we lost. We were insulated on purpose to maintain focus and purpose.

Our road trips on the bus were difficult at times. So, we needed to find ways to pass the time. Barbara, Joan Joyce and others loved playing cards on the bus during our road trips—but that was not for me since I found it too boring.

There was always a mystique about the Brakettes franchise. But it can be easily explained by the tremendous support we received from the Brakette organization and the hard work and the winning attitude of the Brakettes players—to never give up and to achieve success at a very high level.

I felt so honored to play for an organization that was 100 percent committed to providing all the necessary resources needed to become champions. This included financial support needed to run a successful operation and fostering an environment to win—and to win with class. This started with the late Raybestos owner and president Bill Simpson, who believed that his women's softball teams would achieve great success. Because of this support and the everyday hard work of very talented players, the Brakette dynasty has withstood the test of time.

Those who played or coached for the Raybestos franchise had doors opened to pursue career opportunities made available as a direct result from being involved with the Raybestos Brakettes Organization.

So many enjoyable experiences—and happy memories!

So, for me, softball means the unique opportunity to play a sport at a very high level with teammates, opponents and people you admire and respect. And to have fun all along.

Carol Spanks, Orange Lionettes

The best times of my life!

Winning our first world championship was, of course, a real thrill and a memory never to be forgotten. This occurred in 1962 when the Orange

Lionettes came out of the loser's bracket to win the next seven games and the championship title.

We had two sets of uniforms, orange with white and white with orange. We lost our second game wearing our orange uniforms, so we never wore them again. We won our next game in our whites, so we never washed them again. We ate at the same place daily and always followed the same route to the ball field. Now, I realize these superstitious habits didn't make us win, but I sure do believe they helped us *believe* in ourselves and that is the key to success. We won against all odds.

The differences in the game being played now compared to when we played are many. Our playing gear consisted of shorts and tops, stirrup socks and regular metal cleats. We never wore helmets, sliding pads or batting gloves. Our catchers wore masks and chest protectors (many did not wear shin guards). There were only wooden bats and white softballs. Our warm-up drills included pepper. If you are not familiar with this drill, please google it.

The memories and the things that I learned along the way are many. But here's what I do know and very much believe. I am super lucky to have been born when I was and to have played when I did. No, we never had the privilege of the Olympics or Pan American games to participate in. But we had one of the most competitive leagues in the country and also very talented players that played on the same team for years at a time. We had players who were in their late thirties and those in their teen years working together. We had a regular fan base. We enjoyed community support in a variety of ways. We traveled mostly by cars in the days of no freeways and without air conditioning during the stifling heat of the summer.

The game was simple but hard.

My years of playing competitive softball were the best times of my life!

CHRISTINA SUTCLIFF, FORMER FAU PITCHER

Christina's recollections of playing for coach Joan Joyce:

> When you signed with FAU you signed for a lifetime of Joan Joyce in your life.

One of my fondest memories of Coach Joyce is listening to all the amazing stories she shared with us during our road trips. When I would hear her talk on road trips or in her office about her career it was an eye-opening experience for me. Also, I remember playing in tournaments and it would take us an hour to get out of the stadium because so many people would approach her and ask for her autograph. We all knew we were playing for someone special!

Coach Joyce was just fun to be around. It's not only what Coach did for us while we were playing, but more importantly what she did for us *after* we stopped playing for her. She always followed my career and kept me under her wing, always looking out for me. She made a point to attend her former players' weddings, visit our children and things like that. It wasn't just a four-year deal with Coach. When you signed with FAU, you signed for a lifetime of her in your life. And I think that's really what made her special. Coach was one of the most important people in my life, and she meant the world to me. She was my mentor, my second mom, and inspired me daily. Coach was part of the reason I continue to coach. I am eternally grateful to have had Coach Joyce in my life!

IRENE SHEA, BRAKETTES AND FALCONS

An invaluable opportunity for me to serve as a positive role model for young girls

I loved playing the game of softball and I knew I had the skills to play at the top level. I felt that the opportunity to play with the best would one day enhance my ability as a teacher. And it did!

The experience of playing with both the legendary Raybestos Brakettes and the Connecticut Falcons proved to be an invaluable opportunity for me to serve as a positive role model for young girls (and women) interested in playing organized sports.

I relished those opportunities!

JACKIE LEDBETTER, FALCONS

Our team drew thousands of fans for each game.

I think the amazing fans and our relationship with them is my fondest memory of playing in Connecticut. We loved the fans, and they loved us. We were kind of like superhumans to them.

Because of our winning reputation, we drew thousands of fans each game, which was great. They knew us by name. It was so exciting playing in front of large crowds and playing up to their expectations.

As a member of the Falcons, our experience playing in China was incredible. The Chinese players were very disciplined. We were there to teach and prepare them for the Olympics. They were pretty good for being new at the game. Another thing I remember is that, at the time, they had no refrigeration, which was a problem. So every meal they would bring out a stack of sliced bread, but nobody would ever eat it. And for the next meal they would do the same, and we wouldn't eat what they brought out. We were not used to the kind of food they would serve. So we were getting really hungry. Brenda Reilly, our Falcons' coach, couldn't take it anymore and kind of lost it. She said she was so hungry and began shoving all the bread in her mouth. Also, Joan Joyce brought her golf clubs to China so she could practice there. But there was no grass in China at that time! So that was a bummer for her!

But, overall, it was such a fun trip filled with a lot of memories.

I was so lucky. I was in the right place, and I was fortunate to have so many wonderful opportunities playing for the legendary Connecticut Falcons.

JOAN JOYCE, BRAKETTES AND FALCONS
(RECOLLECTIONS BASED ON ONE OF THE AUTHOR'S CONVERSATIONS WITH JOANIE)

I have no regrets. I accomplished everything I wanted to accomplish and I'm proud of my achievements as an athlete. But mainly I am proud of all my teammates, and the "kids" I have the privilege to coach throughout my career.

Growing up in Waterbury, Connecticut, afforded me the opportunity to learn and play a variety of sports, including softball, basketball and volleyball. Because Waterbury was such a sports-minded city in those days, I had no problem playing various sports on girls' teams. Unfortunately, I was not allowed to play baseball because of the ban on women at the time, but I did manage to play most other sports in the Waterbury parks These experiences allowed me to fine-tune my athletic skills at a very young age and prepared me for my future career in sports.

I really didn't realize how fortunate I was to have all these opportunities that Waterbury provided until I spoke to other athletes later on who told me that they never had those opportunities growing up.

JOE JOYCE JR. (BROTHER OF JOAN JOYCE)

The word that best describes Joan both as a person and as an athlete is generous.

The Brakettes and the Connecticut Falcons were outstanding teams. None better. I had the good fortune of watching these amazing athletes many times because my sister pitched for both teams.

Joanie and I played a lot of softball and basketball in the parks in Waterbury, Connecticut. When we were very little, our dad would take Joanie and myself to all his softball (and basketball) games. During batting practice, the guys on deck that were due up next to bat would always leave their gloves on the bench nearby. And so either Joanie or I would grab the glove and go to the outfield to catch fly balls. And always when the batter would finish hitting, he would ask, "Where the heck is my glove?" and someone would shout, "One of the Joyce kids must have it!"

My family made a point to go to all of Joanie's games. One of the most amazing games I saw was when the Brakettes played Japan for the world championship before a sold-out stadium. None of the Japanese players wanted to strike out against Joanie, so every one of the batters bunted against her! I never saw anything like that! Talk about respect for a pitcher!

The word that best describes Joan both as a person and as an athlete is generous. Joanie went out of her way to share her time, expertise, energy and hospitality with others. Joan was a truly dedicated player, coach, sister, aunt and friend.

JOHN STRATTON, BRAKETTES COACH, MANAGER

Micki Stratton was a wonderful person and my best friend.

My fondest memory of the Brakettes was (and is) just being around such wonderful and talented athletes. Every game is a treat. Also traveling with the team, whether within the United States or in Europe, has always been memorable.

My wife, Micki Stratton, was a great catcher for the Brakettes. Micki was a terrific hitter and a great teammate. She was a great "slapper" and bunter.

Micki was the first Brakette to be inducted into the National Softball Hall of Fame, which says a lot. More importantly, Micki was a wonderful person and my best friend.

I remember catching Joan Joyce during practice. She was so accurate. I would put my glove down and tell her to hit the glove. Well, she would hit the glove nine times out of ten, and I would ask her, "How come you didn't make ten out of ten?" She would get so mad and then make sure she did make ten out of ten. That's how competitive she was.

Micki and Joanie were very close friends, and they both were instigators of certain pranks played on us. I remember we were on the road and Joe Barber was the Brakettes general manager. Micki and Joanie went into his room and took everything in the room and shoved it into his shower—mattresses, pillows, everything! When Joe walked into his room, there was absolutely nothing in the room—it was all in the shower! After that, I told several of the girls, "Don't let anyone in my room."

The girls had a lot of fun on the road—water balloon fights, things like that.

In 1996, the Brakettes got a new sponsor. His name was Dr. David O. Carpenter. He was a businessman from Westport. At the time, he owned two Minor League baseball teams. He had never seen a women's fast-pitch softball game. He enjoyed the game so much that he sold the baseball teams and concentrated his time on the Brakettes. He absolutely loved the game, and he loved the Brakettes team. Unfortunately, failing health shortened his tenure with the team. He once told me, "Women's fast-pitch softball is a perfect game, and I hope it never changes." I feel the same way.

JOYCE COMPTON, BRAKETTES AND FALCONS

We knew we had the best pitcher in the world on the mound.

When I played for the Brakettes and the Falcons, we would always kid around and tease each other. I can remember when one of the girls carried an extra bra in her sports bag. Well, we knew Joanie always left her glove in the same spot in the dugout before putting it on to go to the mound. So, we stuffed her glove with this bra. So, when Joanie got to the mound and put her hand in the glove, she takes out this bra on the pitcher's mound and looks at us and starts to crack up on the mound! Joan Joyce was the absolute best—especially in pressure situations!

I recall the two games we had to win to earn the 1974 national championship. Those were both high-pressure games because we had to dig ourselves out of the loser's bracket and needed to win both of those games. Despite the pressure, Joan was simply outstanding, pitching every inning of both of those games to lead us to the 1974 championship. She was a terrific teammate, which made us all feel good. We knew we had the best pitcher in the world on the mound, so if we scored one run, we felt that was usually enough.

People sometimes would refer to us as "JJ and company." We liked to say it was "company and JJ," and Joan preferred it that way. She never sought notoriety at all. Joan was the most competitive person I've ever known. Everything you read about her probably doesn't touch the surface of what she actually did. We didn't have the media coverage that you have now. Despite the lack of coverage, both the Brakettes and Falcons were widely known throughout the United States, and our teams attracted thousands of fans to the games. And if we did have media coverage back then, Joan Joyce would certainly be a household name everywhere—and people would understand why she is referred to as the greatest female athlete in sports history.

Kathy Strahan, Brakettes

An incredible journey

Being part of the Brakettes was truly an incredible experience. For me, it was an experience that set me up for a career in coaching softball at the collegiate level.

Growing up in Lansing, Michigan, I was fortunate to have very supportive parents who realized very early on that I was highly active and saw that every sport I tried came very easily to me.

What I eventually discovered was that I loved to play softball, and I became very good at it. I had a phenomenal playing experience with the Lansing Laurels and Raybestos Brakettes, as well as Team USA in the 1978 World Tournament and 1979 Pan American Games.

As a youngster growing up playing with the Lansing Laurels softball team, it was a dream of mine to play for the Brakettes. And then one day the Brakettes manager Ralph Raymond called me up and asked me to join the team!

I am eternally grateful to all of the people that made my dream a reality. Ralph Raymond, John Stratton and other staff members created a culture that was second to none. Memories and bonds with teammates are forever etched in my mind. The fans in Stratford made being a part of this organization something even more special. It was an incredible journey, and I was blessed to be a part of it all.

During the five years I played with the Brakettes (1977–81), three of the tallest softball pitchers at the time (Kathy Arendsen, Barb Reinalda and Diane "Schuie" Schumacher) were on the team. Each of them stood about six feet tall and were incredibly intimidating on the mound.

At that time, the pitching distance in women's major fast-pitch softball was forty feet. They each threw underhand at speeds around sixty to sixty-five miles per hour. So if you think about their stride length off the pitching rubber and the speed of a sixty-to-sixty-five-mile-per-hour pitch, they could be overwhelmingly intimidating to face as a hitter.

As the shortstop on the team, it was challenging for me at times to stay keenly focused on the batter at the plate, which was very important to do in order to get a good jump on a ground ball upon contact. The reason for this is that there were so many swings and misses from batters flailing at the pitches thrown. So, I found myself constantly fighting off a trance-like state. All three of them were incredibly fun to watch, unless you were on the other team! It was an honor to play with them, and they are perhaps the biggest reason we were so successful. I have no doubt that some of their strikeout records and numbers of no-hitters pitched still stand today.

In 1978, when we represented the United States in the world tournament held in El Salvador, Kathy, Barb and Schuie were the center of attention. Nowhere on any other team in the tournament was a pitching staff that tall, let alone that good. Everyone (fans and players alike) just stared at them. Well, the stares turned into enchantment once the games began, and people saw what they could do on the mound—the speed at which they threw, the movement of their pitches, the strikeouts they recorded. They were nearly unhittable! Our pitching staff was the talk of the tournament, and everyone wanted to watch Team USA play. And it was so exciting winning the world tournament that year. Throughout our time in El Salvador, people wanted their pictures taken with the team, and I just loved watching it all unfold. It was truly a heartwarming experience to see people come together from different countries and to find a common bond and enchantment in our sport.

I eventually took my love of the game into college athletics and put together a thirty-year career as a major college softball coach.

I am retired now. But looking back, I was so fortunate to find something I was good at and built an incredible, wonderful life in the sport of softball.

Kristine Botto Drust

You are now in a very small percentage of the best softball players in the world.
—John Stratton, Brakettes manager

When I first joined the Brakettes, there was one very big moment for me, one that I will never forget. We were at our practice just before the season was about to begin, and I was quite nervous. Our manager, John Stratton, began to hand out these gray jerseys with the word Brakettes in red letters. When he finished passing out the shirts to all the players, John then said to all of us, "Now think very clearly before you decide to put that shirt on. When you put that jersey on, you are now in a very small percentage of the best softball players in the world. Don't put that jersey on if you're not ready to act, walk, talk, prepare and be a Brakette." When he said that, my jaw dropped, because at that moment I truly realized the significance of what he just said and the importance of becoming a part of the Brakettes organization. I have to say if there was one influential moment as a Brakette, it was that practice and the message our manager conveyed to all of us. I never took what he said lightly, and the significance of John's words will always stay with me.

As a coach, I think about the level of excellence of the girls I have had the good fortune of coaching throughout the years. These are players who held themselves to a different standard than any other team I was associated with. I think of their high levels of character, their great work ethic, their winning attitude—which in turn make long seasons seem short. Being part of the Brakettes is not just about softball—it's about the relationships we have formed, our common bond, and the friendships we have preserved—it's about the life lessons we all have learned.

And, of course, I have the utmost respect and admiration of all the players in the past who have worn the Brakettes uniform, especially all the Brakette pioneers.

I am so fortunate to be a part of this legendary sports organization and so proud to be a Brakette!

LINDA FINELLI, BRAKETTES

Playing for the Brakettes was a once-in-a-lifetime experience.

When I first saw Joan Joyce play for the Brakettes, I knew immediately I wanted to be like her. Never did I dream I would be playing on the same team as her! It was a dream come true.

For me, it all started when I was eleven years old watching fast-pitch softball games in the Waterbury Parks League. My dad and Joanie's dad played for the same team, the Waterbury Bombers. I was the bat girl for many of their games, and I closely observed how they played the game.

My rookie season with the Raybestos Brakettes was in 1971. It was a magical year for me because it was the year that the Brakettes had an undefeated season (57-0). That entire season and my entire career with the Brakettes were so much fun. I never thought I would have four of the greatest years of my life.

Rookies were assigned chores such as polishing spikes and washing and ironing uniforms. When the team was in Orlando, JoAnn Cackowski and I gathered up all the uniforms and spikes. We stayed up way past midnight polishing spikes and washing and ironing all the team uniforms.

We decided to deliver the spikes and uniforms door to door very early in the morning, at 6:00 a.m. We knew everyone was sleeping, but for us that was the fun part. The first door we knocked on was Donna Lopiano's room. She came to the door all sleepy eyed and called out, "Do you know what time it is?" We responded, "We sure do!" Then we threw the uniforms into her room and ran, laughing the entire time.

I remember being scared to death on my first plane ride, flying with the Brakettes to Florida. Knowing it was my first plane ride and how scared I was, the team presented me with an air sickness bag—signed by every player on the team. My teammates were a bunch of pranksters. Not only did they each sign the bag, but they made sure to write sayings like, "If all fails, jump." I still have the bag today, which is over fifty years old.

In 1972, the Brakettes traveled to the Intercontinental Games in Calabria, Italy, where we won the gold medal. We spent a few days in Rome sightseeing (Coliseum, Vatican, Trevi Fountain), then off to Salerno, where we took a ski lift ride.

We then flew to Calabria on a thirty-seater propeller airplane. I was terrified, and I'm sure there were others because it was a very bumpy, noisy ride. I was sure at that point that I'd never see my family again. John

Stratton did nothing but laugh the entire time. Pat Harrison was such fun. She received an Italian greeting when in Italy, not sure she was happy about it though. JoAnn Cackowski and I met two Italian guys that wanted to come back to America with us.

Bus trips on our softball tours meant card games—serious card games. I don't remember any card games that I won. Joan Joyce was an amazing card player and rarely lost. Good old fashion game of pitch (setback).

Spring training was tough. Running the bases and being timed, lining up on the first base line and jumping over that line back and forth, infield and outfield drills, playing pepper, hitting and throwing practice. But we did manage to sneak away to the tunnel to sneak a smoke, much to the dislike of Coach Raymond.

In my opinion, we were the sharpest team. Satin uniforms that were made by a seamstress personally for every player. She measured us and made our uniforms. I felt, wow this is pretty cool. You felt special, sort of like royalty.

The fans at Raybestos field were second to none, and they were so kind to us. The very popular Toto's Corner had more food than any restaurant around and shared the food with everyone.

Parties after winning national tournaments were the best. Hotel swimming pools, food and soda and celebrating all together. Coming back from national tournaments and landing in New York, we were met with police escorts on our way to Raybestos Field, where we were met by legions of fans and the press.

Playing softball for the Brakettes was just a fun time for all of us. There was always laughter and plenty of jokes. Those lighter moments sure helped us wind down so that when gametime approached we were better able to focus our attention on the game at hand—and on winning.

When you played for the Raybestos Brakettes you were told to never disrespect that uniform. We stood for the flag. We traveled everywhere, and wherever we traveled we were asked to be ambassadors for our team and the sport of softball. Playing for the Brakettes taught me respect for our country and the Brakettes organization.

Signing autographs was an important part of being a Brakette (before and after games), especially for the young children. And all of us took this very seriously since we were fully aware of the fact that many young girls (and boys) had the same aspirations as we had when we were their age. We knew that many young children looked up to us as role models. We all felt that we needed to push forward so these young children could see how the sport of softball was meant to be played.

For me, playing for the Brakettes was a once-in-a-lifetime experience. An undefeated season in my rookie season, four national championships during my four years, an intercontinental championship and the 1974 World Title against Japan. A lifetime of memories—and just plain fun. It just doesn't get much better than that.

I was so fortunate to have the opportunity to play for such a wonderful softball organization and to have the support of such extremely talented, caring teammates! The camaraderie amongst the players was immeasurable—no matter if you were a starter on the field or a substitute. There were always lessons to be learned, friendships to cultivate and experiences not to be forgotten. When all is said and done, we were all one big family.

Softball, indeed, helped me grow as a woman.

MARGIE WRIGHT, ST. LOUIS HUMMERS AND FSU HEAD COACH

Every dream I ever had as a kid came true.

After a fifty-year-career of playing and coaching softball I decided to retire in 2013.

Even though there were many difficult times fighting the Title IX battles and fighting for opportunities to use my God-given talents, I wouldn't trade them for anything in the world.

I would like to share an example of how Joan Joyce inspired me and so many other athletes during her amazing career.

Joanie taught me a knuckleball change up in 1974. At the time, she was a referee at the AIAW National Basketball Championship in NC. Still in her referee outfit, Joanie brought me to a gym and taught me the changeup. I even got her out on that pitch a few times in the Pro League. That's how generous she was—to go out of her way and teach me a pitch that I would use effectively against her.

Joanie was my inspiration to be a AIAW referee for large college women's basketball, and I got to ref two National Championships.

Every dream I ever had as a kid came true: a national champion, an Olympic champion, becoming the winningest softball coach in the NCAA, graduating all the athletes I was fortunate to coach and making my family proud that I took advantage of every opportunity.

Such wonderful memories!

MARY LOU PENNINGTON, SAN JOSE SUNBIRDS

I love team sports and enjoyed every minute of fast-pitch softball.

There is no denying the Connecticut Falcons were the best team in the league. Joan Joyce, Irene Shea, Willie Roze and Joyce Compton were the best at their position. What struck me most about the Falcon players was that they let their talent speak for itself. No bragging, no boasting—just going out there and playing the game the best that it could be played.

I had both the opportunity to play against and with the talented pitcher Charlotte Graham. Charlotte was a pitcher for the San Jose Sunbirds as well as other teams of the WPS league. When I played against her, I didn't like her much. I thought she had too much of a fiery personality. When we became teammates, I realized how wrong I was. She was such a competitor and was passionate about the game. We formed a special bond as batterymates. One I will cherish forever.

After playing for the Santa Clara Laurels, I had the honor of playing in the WPS league for the San Jose Sunbirds, Santa Ana Lionettes and the NY Golden Apples.

I enjoyed playing on all the teams I was on. I love team sports.

I enjoyed every minute of fast-pitch softball.

PAT HARRISON, BRAKETTES

How does a kid get so lucky?

My career in sports was one of wonder and amazement. To say it was magical would be an understatement. None of it was really planned. Looking back, it all just seemed to happen. I do know that it happened because I was willing to put one foot in front of the other to satisfy my desire to participate at the highest level possible for me.

So many players and coaches supported my journey. Teammates were always so essential to my success on the field. When I was scared or I didn't feel I was good enough, they carried the load until I was able to ground myself and remember that I was capable of completing the task at hand.

When I was sixteen years old, I began my Senior A career as a member of the South Hill Queens at South Memorial Park in Vancouver, British Columbia, Canada. The legendary Shirley Topley was our player/coach. How does a kid get so lucky?

In 1960, we were invited to the ASA World Championship in Stratford, Connecticut. This was my first exposure to Raybestos Memorial Field and to the Raybestos Brakettes. The world of women's softball was presented to me like a banquet or a smorgasbord, free to experience everything the world of softball had to offer.

Talented teams from all over the United States and two from Canada were at Raybestos Field. Players such as Joan Joyce, Bertha Ragan Tickey, Micki (Macchietto) Stratton, Dot Wilkinson, Billie Harris, Carol Spanks, Nance Ito, Sis King, Loreene Ramsey, Carolyn Fitzwater, Lois Williams, Hap Piper, Jeanne Contel, Gloria May and so many more talented women. This was the beginning of my deep desire to return to this hub of softball and to be part of the Raybestos magic.

At the tournament, my Vancouver teammates and I were sitting in the outfield bleachers. Next to us was the team from Tennessee. Nera White, Tennessee's All-American basketball star, was engaged in a conversation with our coach, Shirley Topley. The topic was the sport of curling. At that time, curling was an obscure sport for most Americans. Shirley, an avid curler in Canada, was trying to explain the game to Nera. At one point, a bewildered Nera, in her deep Tennessee drawl, shouted out, "You mean they throw twenty-five-pound boulders down a piece of ice, and then they sweep the boulder with a broom? How in the world is that a sport?!" For us Canadians, Nera's "understanding" of the sport of Curling was priceless!

In 1961, the ASA World Championship was held in Portland, Oregon. Once again, Vancouver was invited. The final game featured the Whittier Gold Socks and the Brakettes. The game did not conclude until three thirty in the morning. Even though everyone was freezing, no one wanted to leave. Fans in the outfield built small fires to stay warm. Whittier's Lou Albrecht versus Stratford's Joan Joyce—WOW. It was an epic battle indeed.

In 1963, the Brakettes won the right to represent USA Softball in the first international "World Tournament" in Melbourne, Australia. The Aussies won in the tournament final, but let me tell my story about that experience.

Bertha Ragan and a seventeen-year-old Donna Lopiano anchored our pitching staff. The umpire in chief (who shall remain anonymous) from the United States was sent to this six-team tournament to assist with rules interpretation since softball was a young sport for the host Aussies and most other teams attending.

Bertha Ragan's figure-eight pitching delivery was probably the most legal of all the pitches in the United States. The Aussie and New Zealand umpires started calling illegal pitches on Bertha. After consulting with the

Rules Interpreter from the ASA, the "umpire-in-chief," knowing it was a legal pitch, decided instead to agree with the rules interpreter, as he did not want to upset or offend the hosts. The result for Bertha meant that she had to change her complete delivery, including how she stood on the mound. This, in turn, caused Bertha to injure her hip. She was now finished for the tournament.

So, enter Donna Lopiano, our rookie pitcher. Donna was young and really unproven up to that point. She was fast and hard to hit but she was a bit wild at times. Donna did manage to get us to the championship game against Australia. But in the seventh inning, an Aussie ended up on second base. Donna then threw a wild pitch that got past Micki and went back to the "makeshift" backstop. This was not a normal backstop. The "backstop" was actually some tangled netting hanging from large poles. The excess netting at the bottom was loosely shoved into a concrete wall. Now, the distance from home plate to the back wall and the netting was at least fifty feet, if not more. (I would guess the normal distance would be maybe twenty feet at best.) Micki ran back to retrieve the ball, and by the time she found it wedged at the bottom of the netting, the runner scored from second base. That was how the game ended. We were not happy about the result or all of the circumstances that led up to it.

While still reeling from the events that occurred during this tournament, a couple of us went to the pharmacy that evening to buy some shaving cream. Someone (not saying who) got the room key of the above-named U.S. "umpire-in-chief." While we had no complaints against the Australia team, we did feel that this pitch decision, which resulted in the injury of our star player, was a big reason for our loss. For not having the conviction to make the correct decision (a decision he knew would have been the correct decision), we decided to touch up his room just a bit! We did a fine job, although no one was sure where he slept that night—oh well!

Each Brakette had a first-class ticket around the world simply because we loved the wonderful game of softball, and we were privileged to be members of a fabulous team called the Raybestos Brakettes.

Ralph Raymond was named the new Brakette manager after joining the coaching staff for the 1966 season. He was intense and challenged us every step of the way. He made it very clear that each of us needed to show up for every game with nothing but our best. And if you didn't bring your best to each game you heard about it, individually or as a team. One of his favorite lines was "you looked like garbage"—now add his Boston accent so that it sounded like he was saying "Gaaawbagggge." It was loud, and when he addressed you individually, all one could do was look at the ground. Sometimes I used to think people in the parking lot could hear every word, but we learned and we worked harder than ever. He motivated us in so many ways. Ralph taught us so many of the little things that make a team successful. We were all learning new tasks, and it was exciting. Ralph would say, "If you pay attention to all of the little things, the game will take care of itself."

I retired in 1972 and returned to Vancouver in 1973, where I began my coaching career, which took me into the 1980s.

I was honored to be inducted into the National Softball Hall of Fame in 1976. Up until Shirley Topley was inducted, I was the only Canadian who received such an important recognition. During my ceremony, what flooded my mind was the hearts of the fans, the hearts of my teammates, the hearts of my opponents and every single individual who had been a part of my Brakettes experience. Thank you, Raybestos!

My coaches have guided me through a career that was like something I could only dream about. My teammates encouraged and supported me, ensuring that I always had a safe landing. My opponents inspired me, challenged me, and some became lifelong friends. The fans—especially at Raybestos Field—took me in and made me feel as though I had been in Stratford all of my life. This was my home away from Vancouver.

Just as important, my softball experiences helped me, as a coach, to inspire and encourage young girls to be a part of this wonderful sport known as softball.

Softball guided the trajectory of my life. It helped me define who I was as a human being and as an athlete. Softball gave me a purpose. I was blessed with the greatest role models and mentors.

This was my personal "Field of Dreams." Today, it is my past to reflect on, to own and to treasure!

PEGGY KELLERS, BRAKETTES

Being a role model on and off the field was important—and an expectation of each Brakette player.

The desire and assumption for the Brakettes every year from our owner Bill Simpson, our fans and our team was to win nationals. The saying "no excuses, just results" often came to my mind. During my eleven seasons, we accomplished that goal seven years and were runners-up the other four years. Winning nationals was such a satisfying, exciting experience, and the off-season was very pleasant. Our coaches instilled in us that the times we did not win the championship (or even when we lost a game during the regular season) that those experiences should be viewed as a learning opportunity rather than a failure. Which I believe is very good advice.

To keep us sharp from game to game during the regular season, a monetary fine system was in place. Physical errors were part of the game, so no fine was incurred for throwing errors, bobbles on defense or missing a grounder or fly. Examples of fines were missing a signal, failure to advance the runner on a sacrifice, throwing to the wrong base and missing cut-offs. Fines imposed usually cost us twenty-five to fifty cents for each incident. In addition, as a team, if the game went into extra innings, all players owed a quarter for each extra inning. The longest game I remember was thirty-two innings against a Perkasie, Pennsylvania team as the nightcap of a doubleheader. (We won both games.) The money was used for an end-of-season party for the team.

With Raybestos as our sponsor and the strong support of Bill Simpson, each Brakette realized how good we had it. When we would hear about other nationally known teams that had to do fundraising, travel in personal vehicles and stay in crowded, inexpensive motels, we were very grateful for our situation. The Brakette organization rented a charter bus for road trips, arranged for flights and rental cars and reserved nice motels with two beds for two players to a room. The trade-off? Win nationals!

Because our reputation was as a highly competitive team and eventually a dynasty, it was important to be motivated for each game. Without sounding cocky, the hardest games to get ready for were against lesser-known or "weaker" teams. We each had a responsibility to be well prepared and motivated for every opponent. The days we overlooked our opponents were the ones in which we either struggled to win or came up short, suffering a loss. It became very apparent that those teams came to play, were hungry for an upset and put it all on the line because they had nothing to lose. Keeping that lesson in the forefront of our minds helped our motivation each time.

When playing top-level teams, opponents and archrivals, getting motivated was never a problem. Deep down, even though we were nervous, we enjoyed the challenge of performing well and learned to welcome tough competition.

We were mindful of what we said during interviews so as not to bad-mouth opposing teams. Ralph Raymond instilled in us what it meant to be a champion. He would remind us to do our talking on the field, between the white lines. Showing respect for teams was important no matter what our personal likes and dislikes were of players. After all, their perceptions of any Brakette may have been very similar!

One time we read an article prior to an away game in which the opposing team referred to our team as "JJ & Company." Joan Joyce ("JJ") was probably the angriest about the label. She was a true team player. As great and successful as she was as a pitcher, she'd be the first to tell you that it took a strong team behind her to win games. The article was an additional motivator for us, and we had fun with it. We ordered gray T-shirts for each player except Joan Joyce with red letters stenciled on the front, "JJ and Company." On the back was "Company." Joan had a red T-shirt with white letters on the front, "JJ and Company." On the back of her shirt was "JJ." We got permission to wear them over our uniforms during warm-ups. The opposing team got the message quickly and probably wanted to withdraw the quote after the significant victory we had against them.

Many people had a strong curiosity about successful female athletes. I enjoyed talking with people about my experiences and opportunities. Because of the status associated with being a Raybestos Brakette, it was obvious that being a role model on and off the field was important and an expectation of each player.

Although the Brakettes didn't necessarily think about being pioneers for our sport, it was a reality in hindsight. We were just grateful to be given the opportunity to play the sport we loved and use our athletic talents in a constructive way.

To keep us motivated throughout the season, we had "Red & White Batting Teams." A captain was appointed for each one, and the two captains split the roster up as evenly as possible at the beginning of the season. During each game, the competition within our team involved having the best team batting average. The losing team in a game each paid fifty cents and carried the equipment to the bus or locker room. As you can imagine, we stayed motivated, rooting for the whole team against our opponent. It was lots of fun and often came down to the last inning to determine the hitting team winner!

In preseason conditioning drills, Ralph Raymond was fairly creative. One that was fun involved relay races doing piggy backs. Because I was a catcher and Ralph wanted my legs to be strong, he always paired me with the heaviest Brakette teammates.

During my first two seasons, I was a reserve catcher and also played second base. In order to learn about calling signals for our pitchers and watching various opposing hitters, I developed a pitching chart system. I recorded every pitch thrown, its type and the outcome (ball, strike swinging, strike called, foul ball, hit, etc.). It helped me watch for any patterns for each pitcher and her strongest pitches against various hitters. In addition, a pitch count was readily available for the coaches. Once I became the starting catcher, I'm not sure whether my back-up catcher appreciated following through on my tedious yet helpful system!

Another fun part of my experience as a catcher was working with each pitcher according to her strengths so that she was an effective, successful pitcher in each outing. During the years when our pitching staff included Donna Hebert, Joan Joyce, Donna Lopiano and Bertha Ragan Tickey, we had the most depth and talent, in my opinion. Each pitcher had different strengths, styles and personalities. I enjoyed the challenge of catching each of them. Routinely catching many perfect games and no-hitters was an exciting and rewarding accomplishment for our battery (pitcher and catcher).

In my early years as a Brakette, some of the veterans were devout Catholics. This was at a time when nuns wore black habits and priests wore white collars with a black top. On our away trips, we made up our own game. If anyone saw a nun or priest, she called it out (using discretion in a restaurant). Follow me now—the player licked her thumb, pressed it into her opposite palm, and punched the wet spot with her other fist. Being the first to see a priest was worth one hit for the upcoming game, whereas two nuns were worth one hit! Got it? Ahh—and the superstitions began!

Players' superstitions were something I learned quickly. For example, whoever had a good night at the plate usually ate the same meal before the next game. Putting one's uniform socks on in the same order was another superstition for some players. When we were scheduled to play the Orange Lionettes, a huge rival, we drank tomato juice (red was our color) for breakfast rather than orange juice!

For our away trips by bus, many players passed the time by playing card games. Our bus driver John made a board that fit in the aisle along four rows of seats. The main games were setback and wild-card rummy with decent money for the winners. It kept several people occupied during the trip. Card games also served to pass the time during free times at the motel.

International travel was very exciting and an opportunity I never would have had at such a young age without being a Brakette. Canada was a standard trip in any given season. Additionally, we spent time in Europe traveling to such places as Holland and Italy. Not only were we there to compete but also to work with opposing players at clinics so that the skill levels of the players in those countries would improve. We worked with teams as far away as Zambia, Africa.

We had a seamstress who made our red and white satin uniforms and travel suits for airplane trips. The uniforms were classy looking and very unique in that the back of the shirt extended so that a piece came in between our legs and buttoned in the front. It kept our shirts tucked in our uniform shorts throughout the game, helping us look neat. We would go to her house for the fitting, and for whatever reason, the reds seemed roomier than the whites. Many players referred to them as "tight whites." The travel suits in the mid-1960s were dressy—red jackets and red skirts. We wore white heels with them. Later in the 1960s, she made a medium blue top with matching slacks, which was much more comfortable.

As a catcher, I would occasionally get hit with a foul ball. My thighs took a beating with a black-and-blue mark from the ball if it hit me there. The tough one was when a foul tip hit my ring finger and pinky on my throwing hand. I was careful to keep that hand in a loose fist with my thumb protected throughout each pitch. What put me in a vulnerable position was when one of our pitchers would not shake off the pitch I called but instead threw a different pitch. For example, if I signaled for a drop pitch, I would be in a position to catch a drop. For one pitcher, when she did not shake me off, I suddenly realized a rise ball was coming after it left her hand. It meant shifting my position. If the batter fouled off the ball it would sometimes hit my two fingers on my throwing hand, causing pain and swelling.

A veteran catcher on our men's team, the Raybestos Cardinals, told me a unique remedy using lemons. On the way back from the game, we stopped at the store to buy two lemons. I would cut off each end and push my finger through each one. To keep the juice from dripping out, I would wrap a towel or ace bandage around my hand. Keeping the lemons on overnight took out the soreness and reduced some of the swelling so I was able to catch the next game.

Speaking at banquets and making hospital visits often came my way because I lived in Stratford. Occasionally, Joe Barber would ask me to visit a Brakette fan who was hospitalized. When I went into the room, the wife was usually there. On one occasion, after introducing myself, the man's innocent reply was, "Oh, I didn't recognize you with clothes on!" It was an awkward "oops" moment, and my response was, "Yes, I probably look different in street clothes rather than my uniform." Naturally, his wife was quite relieved, and we had a good laugh. Since it happened more than once, I came to expect that type of comment. The people were so surprised and grateful that a Brakette would come in for a visit.

Interviews by reporters after our games occasionally tended to be awkward moments. Many male reporters seemed to struggle with the types of questions they should ask our teammates. They would ask silly questions, such as, "Are Brakettes allowed to wear makeup during their games?" or "Are the Brakette girls allowed to get married?" Keep in mind that many of us played during a male-dominated, chauvinistic period of time.

My first funeral came when our honorary batgirl lost her battle with cancer. Her family were longtime supporters of the Brakettes. Nancy Sulzicki (about eleven or twelve years old) had lost one leg above her knee because of a tumor. Nancy became our honorary batgirl one season. We all enjoyed having her with us at home games. It was sad when we lost her. Attending my first-ever visitation as a teenager was extremely difficult, even though the family was so grateful that I came on behalf of the Brakettes organization.

Pat Walker of the Orlando Rebels knew I would visit my grandmother in Florida during the off-season. Pat would ask me to do hospital visits with her. Because the Rebels were one of our arch "enemies" on the field, visiting with a Rebel fan or player provided its own set of comments. It was usually all in good fun, and I know that a visit by "a Brakette" brought out the human side of competitors "off the field."

The toughest visitation for me was when a young, outstanding former Falcon outfielder was diagnosed with MS. Although I had retired from the game by then, I knew who Kathy Stilwell was. When Pat Harrison took me to visit her, I was very grateful for the opportunity. We each were very religious people, so our conversation also included prayer. Several months later, when I heard that Kathy lost her battle to MS, it was a very difficult sense of loss for the softball world and me.

The Raybestos Brakettes were well known throughout Connecticut. Thousands would attend our regular-season home games. When we played for nationals and world tournaments, the standing-room-only fans were estimated at over fifteen thousand people.

In other parts of the country, we would often draw the largest crowds for the home team, which gave their team some well-deserved recognition. We also played in several goodwill benefit games for organizations such as the Shriners and Jimmy Fund. It was good for our sport and for the specific benefit. Often we were considered goodwill ambassadors for the sport of softball—a label none of us took lightly.

When our away games were in city parks or on other fields, there were no fences. Our team would get caught up in the long-fly-ball syndrome in which the outfielders would be really deep and our long fly balls ended up being an easy out. Coach Raymond would adamantly encourage us to go for line drives for more success. My point in writing this is that our home run statistics would have been much higher and also our batting averages if we had always played exclusively in the stadiums with fences.

One of our fun traditions was jumping in the hotel swimming pool after winning nationals. (The hotel guests didn't appreciate or understand the late-night noise coming from the pool!) When Raybestos hosted the tournament, our team stayed at a hotel in Milford, Connecticut. No matter where nationals were held, we never stayed in the tournament hotel where the other fifteen teams were housed. I'm sure it rubbed those teams the wrong way, but it was another example of the support Bill Simpson gave us as our sponsor.

There were no hats or T-shirts handed out to the national champions on the field after winning. We did receive trophies that night and championship rings later on. Players named to the first and second All-American Team received plaques. Oh, and the president didn't invite us to the White House either. After winning the national and world championship in 1974, President Ford did send us each a congratulatory letter.

One year, Donna Lopiano brought a new Polaroid camera to practice. What was unique about this was that one click of the camera produced an eight-frame sequence instantly. It was an amazing piece of technology at the time, and we used it to analyze our hitters' swinging and pitchers' delivery motion. In that day, video cameras were not available, and probably no one owned an 8-millimeter camera.

Analyzing our pitchers' deliveries, we discovered that because of Joan Joyce's additional rotation and shoulder flexibility, she actually had much more leverage than other pitchers, making her pitches jump so much. Her innate, God-given abilities and athletic prowess were amazing!

Pitching machines had not been invented in that era. Oh, how many of us would have benefitted from using one! At one point, a teammate had seen a demonstration of a device used to practice hitting. A player would stand holding a wooden bat upright in her hands. A rope was securely attached to the top of the bat, and on the other end of the rope was a softball. A hook was drilled into the ball so that the rope could be securely attached. She would twirl the rope while keeping the bat upright near her body. At a distance beyond the length of the rope a hitter would stand with a bat. When facing the direction the ball was coming, she hit it. The ball went back in a circular trajectory. As the twirler got better, she moved the ball in an upward trajectory to replicate a rise ball or at the height of the player's knees to practice a low pitch. For pitches inside and outside, it was up to the batter to move accordingly. Of course, all of this is archaic compared to the amazing devices they have now. But we used what we could create—it's all we had.

During the early days of softball, it was one of the few sports available and accessible to women, since they were banned from baseball and other activities. No one was required to join a club with membership fees such as for golf and tennis. Therefore, it was a relatively inexpensive sport to participate in.

Top-level women's softball was (and is) a fast-paced, entertaining game. In Stratford, Connecticut, for example, the women's games outdrew the men's games by a significant margin. Many fans prefer the fast-paced, "no nonsense, let's just play" aspect compared to the men's slower, methodical routines of pitchers and hitters after every pitch modeled by MLB. And they can also see that the females, even during the game, had fun and would cheer their teammates on throughout the game—no matter what the score.

WILLIE ROZE, BRAKETTES, FALCONS

I learned there was a place for women in sports and that I was a small part of it.

I was fortunate to play for the Brakettes from 1965 to 1975, and I am so proud of our many team accomplishments. We won eight of ten national titles, and at one point, it was five in a row. We even had an undefeated season in 1971.

In 1974, we won the national and world championships. The world championship was played in front of over fifteen thousand screaming fans. I was lucky enough to contribute the game-winning double, and I felt such pride in representing the United States. It was not the Olympics, but it was as close as I would ever get.

Looking back, I realize how fortunate I was to play with some truly outstanding people and how important our personal interactions were.

I remember my rookie treatment—rooms ransacked, having to clean and shine veteran players' shoe spikes and also doing their laundry. On my first major road trip, I was advised that I would need to purchase white gloves and a hat to go with our newly made travel outfits. I was sure it was a joke, but was it? Sure enough, when Brenda Riley and Ann DeLuca came to pick me up, they were outfitted with hats and gloves. They carried the ruse all the way to the airport, where they finally fessed up! Just to be safe, I had purchased my hat and gloves! Of course, it was all in good fun. So many fun memories!

If I have one regret, it is that softball was never included in the Olympics during my playing time. For years, it had been discussed, and it finally occurred in 1996. I would have loved to represent the United States in the Olympics.

One major highlight of my career was being inducted into the ASA National Softball Hall of Fame in 1985.

I got to play against some of the great teams and great players. I was blessed to play for some awesome coaches and with many very talented teammates. I learned that with hard work you can accomplish anything.

More importantly, I learned there was a place for women in sports and that I was a small part of it. It's nice to see how far we've come in that respect!

I fondly reminisce about my playing days—of championships won, of timely hits and some defensive plays and of all my teammates and friends. And, oh, what about the great fans!

I have so many wonderful memories of my days spent at the old ballpark—and I would do it all again in a heartbeat!

12

PLAYERS' ADVICE TO YOUNG GIRLS (AND WOMEN) WHO WOULD LIKE TO EXCEL IN FAST-PITCH SOFTBALL

Women, especially young girls, need positive role models if they wish to be successful in the world of sports and, more importantly, in the world of life.
—*Irene Shea, Brakettes and Falcons*

Author's note: I asked some former fast-pitch softball players (and coaches) to share their thoughts and provide advice to young girls (possibly preteens)—who dream of becoming a member of a softball team and perhaps a future softball superstar—and also parents of these young girls.

Here are their responses:

DIANE "SCHUIE" SCHUMACHER

- Be willing to be coachable by making adjustments as you develop your skills, especially because you may have a variety of coaches throughout your levels of play.
- Learn the game by watching fast-pitch softball on TV and in person.
- Be observant.
- Observe the HOWS: How the catch is made, how a throw is made, how to make contact with the bat on the ball.
- Observe the WHYS: Why certain plays are executed on the field or why the hit and run or bunt is executed in a situation.
- Learn to know WHAT you are doing when you field a ball, throw, hit, run, slide, so you can eventually make self-corrections.

Brakette Cassie Ruscz with batgirls, 2015. *Courtesy of Brakettes Photo Archive.*

- Be patient with your mistakes, since mistakes are nothing but learning opportunities.
- If you want to be the best, you have to be willing to sacrifice.
- Go where the best coaches are.
- The best competition is to challenge yourself.
- You not only should have a love for the game but a passion for the game of softball. If you do, you will play for a long time.
- If you need a break from playing and practicing, you may want to take a year off to recharge your desire and passion.
- Stay physically, mentally and emotionally healthy throughout your journey.
- Most mistakes at the higher levels are the result of not being emotionally steady. Bad decisions and poor execution are sometimes due to fear of failing, fear of making a mistake. Remember mistakes should be looked at as learning opportunities. Confidence is the best way to overcome the fear of the unknown.
- Be your best self!
- Thrive in pressure situations.
- Be competitive but always have fun!
- Remember there is no pressure if you are prepared.
- Always be a good teammate.

Advice for the parent of the child:

- Be involved as a supporter of your child.
- Be ready to have teachable moments with your child throughout her journey.
- Observe your child in winning and losing moments.
- Immediately after a game, avoid going over the mistakes until the next day. Ask them what they learned about the game they played. What kind of improvements are needed.
- Go have ice cream, as you never see an unhappy child eating ice cream. That's what my dad did after every game as a child, win or lose. He coached me at nine and ten.
- Parents can be involved, can influence, but never should interfere with their child's learning process in sports.
- Enjoy your child's journey, as it is a special time to create a long-lasting bond of love and support as well as memories that last a lifetime.

Advice for a coach:

- Coach the player where they are. You don't coach the sport. You coach girls who play the sport. It is their game now not yours.
- Teach them to think, to learn and understand the game.
- Teach them to respect the game, their opponents and each other.
- Let your catchers call the game, especially at the higher levels.
- Teach your catchers how to call pitches at the high school level.
- Teach your pitchers too.
- Keep your signals simple. Your players should not need a wristband to look at if you keep your signals simple. Your players should not have to look at their pitching coaches for each pitch (I hate this in today's game at the college level.)
- Also share the history of this game. Who were the players and great coaches before them? Learn about their struggles, hard work and how they overcame so many adversarial conditions they were faced with. It is these softball pioneers who made it possible for young girls to dream about playing softball on a team, especially fast-pitch softball at a high level.
- Keep learning by reading books, watching TV, asking questions of successful softball coaches and attending softball clinics.

- Keep it fun. It can be fun to learn, fun to win, fun to improve. Losing is not fun, but the discovery of how they lost can be fun when a coach interacts with their players to gauge their knowledge and how they react to a loss.
- "Sports womanship" is important.
- You can always learn something to bring back to your team.

IRENE SHEA

It is my belief that young girls who aspire to be part of a team, and possibly a softball star, should have a deep appreciation of the athletes who came before them, especially the very talented pioneers of the game of softball. It is these pioneers who, through their hard work and struggles, made it possible for girls to now dream of becoming the next softball superstar.

My advice to young girls who are interested in becoming a successful fast-pitch softball player is this. Always remember the three Cs: (1) COURAGE to make your choice of sport (2) COMMITMENT to the hard work required (3) CONFIDENCE to be the best you can.

And be sure to practice hard, listen to your coach's advice, have confidence in your ability, be a good teammate and, most importantly, have fun!

JACKIE LEDBETTER

- Just keep playing. Like in San Diego, we would take November off but then play all year round. So, keep playing.
- Do well in school.
- Listen to your coaches, and do what they say.
- Keep going through the ranks. And have fun doing it.
- And even when you graduate from high school, you may not be able to become a professional but you can get a scholarship to college. Education is most important.
- Not everyone is destined to become a professional softball player. But you sure can have fun trying.

Jane Blalock, Golfing Great, Co-owner of Falcons

- Play all sports, don't focus on one sport.
- Be a kid and have fun.
- The game will be there forever.
- Enjoy your childhood and play the game because you enjoy it, not because your parents want you to play.
- And practice as much as you can.

Joan Joyce
(taken from July 2, 2018 interview and from personal discussions)

I don't know that I would have liked playing one sport all year long. I worked very hard to be successful at a variety of sports. I enjoyed the challenge that each sport presented. That's what made things interesting and fun for me. It gave me a fresh outlook on each sport, on my wonderful teammates and on life itself.

- I would advise young girls to play a variety of sports, love those sports and work really hard on those sports.
- Besides softball, the child should be involved in other sports such as basketball, volleyball, soccer, until at least she is out of high school.
- Be an all-around athlete.
- But be a kid. Have fun.
- And you have to love every sport you are involved in. You need to have passion for the sport of fast-pitch softball in order to be successful.
- Learn by doing, but don't involve yourself in only one sport twelve months out of the year.

Advice to parents of young children:

- Confidence, determination and self-esteem are vitally important for young girls in sports—and in life. Learn how your child can overcome their fears by having confidence. True confidence and determination are absolutely necessary if the child wants to become a successful athlete. And most of all, help them develop self-esteem—understand that they have the ability to overcome all the obstacles that they will face in sports (and in life). But they really have to work at it. Confidence, determination and self-esteem are things that people are not born with. That's where you come in as a supportive parent. I was so blessed to have very supportive parents who taught me self-esteem at a very, very early age. They did this by both words and actions. Once your child learns these important traits, she will not only benefit in sports but, more importantly, in the world of life!

JOHN STRATTON, BRAKETTES MANAGER

- I always tell my players when they first come up that I would rather them do something right once than something a thousand times wrong.
- Hard work doesn't necessarily mean breaking a sweat. Doing it right is the hard work.
- Make your motion perfect; make your spin perfect. Same thing with hitting. Never swing up; never be late on the swing; swing even and level. Simple things like that. Learn to do it right and do it right every single time.
- Do it right once than a thousand times wrong.

JOYCE COMPTON

- Just be a kid.
- Don't limit yourself to one sport. That is so important to me.
- Do what you enjoy doing.
- Work hard, practice, but have fun.
- If you don't have fun playing the sport, don't do it.
- We had fun.

KATHY STRAHAN

- If you love the game, play different positions to get a better feel and understanding of what is involved. For example, if you have been learning how to play second base, spend some time taking ground balls at shortstop or third base to get a better feel for that side of the infield. You might also try a little time in the outfield.
- After you get comfortable with a certain position and enjoy being there, work hard to improve your skills.
- Study the game.
- Work on all facets of the offense—not just swinging away and hitting a pitch, but sacrifice bunting, squeeze bunting and drag bunting.
- Practice, practice, practice.
- Find a team where you live—one that is a good fit—and learn how to compete.
- I think your journey from there will take care of itself.
- If you have a dream to be a softball star, chase it. Because that dream won't chase you back.

Advice for the parent of the child:

- Encourage your daughter to chase her dreams and spend time with her to do just that.
- My mother and father were so supportive of my softball journey that started at a very young age. They spent time with me playing catch in the backyard and tossing whiffle balls to me to hit. As I became more skilled, they could see I was standing out compared to other girls my age. So they took me to a local softball clinic offered by a really good local women's softball team, the Lansing Laurels, in my hometown of Lansing, Michigan. The manager of the team recognized my talent immediately and spoke to my parents about allowing me to attend team practices.
- As a parent, you will see the development of skills and a genuine enthusiasm from your daughter in doing them. As you see specific skills take hold, add to them.
- These days, there are youth softball teams, sophisticated travel ball teams and college softball teams that put on youth clinics to teach young people specific softball skills. Take advantage of these opportunities.

- There are also private hitting and pitching coaches, softball training facilities and various avenues that will lead to playing the game of softball.
- Open the door, and see what's on the other side!

KRISTINE BOTTO DRUST

I have a seven-year-old daughter who absolutely loves playing softball. I have photos of her and her teammates. The photos are of pure glory and smiles, loving the game and her teammates. That's the fun part—the relationships you acquire, being part of something bigger than yourself and working together to have a sense of purpose.

My advice to young girls who would like to excel in softball is to learn everything about the game and everything it has to offer—all the fun, frustrations, winning as well as losing. Learn how successful players deal with failure, because failure is part of the game. Learn all the positions, not just one position, because that will make you a more valuable player.

As you get older, learn how to say "yes" if an important opportunity arises, such as trying out for a more advanced team, even if it means more work and more of a commitment.

Study the game. Don't just play the game. If you love playing softball and if you are passionate about the game, it will make you a better player and a more compassionate person.

Learn to be a good teammate and how to show respect for your fellow players and your competitors. Practice because you want to and not because you have to. When you feel all your preparation start to work, that's when you will realize that all your hard work is beginning to pay off and it's the first step to becoming a successful player.

LINDA FINELLI

My advice to young girls who dream of joining a fast-pitch softball team is for you to always follow your dreams.

You should always play to the best of your ability, even when obstacles present themselves (and they will).

Learn to trust your ability and have the confidence to overcome those obstacles. Practice as much as you are allowed. And always take the advice of *supportive* parents, teachers and coaches.

You may not become a softball superstar (not many achieve that goal), but the life lessons you will learn from playing softball and forming bonds with your teammates are immeasurable.

MARGIE WRIGHT, ST. LOUIS HUMMERS

- I am grateful for all the females before me who made it possible for women like me to have success in this sport that we love and cherish.
- You should make a point to understand and appreciate the struggles and the accomplishments of softball players who came before you, especially the very talented pioneers. Learn about their struggles and sacrifices, which made it possible for young girls to even dream of becoming a part of a softball team and possibly becoming a softball superstar. What were their secrets in overcoming adversities and becoming very successful in the world of fast-pitch softball, and in life?
- I hope that the stories and advice of many of these former softball players will motivate young girls with big dreams to simply take the challenge of becoming very good at fast-pitch softball.
- Just go for it!

MARY LOU PENNINGTON, SAN JOSE SUNBIRDS

- If you are blessed to play a sport at a high level, always remember it is a God-given talent.
- Be humble and let your actions speak for you.
- Go out there and play that game, and enjoy that game!
- Young girls now have so many opportunities waiting for them.
- Get your education, maybe get a scholarship.
- Practice, practice, practice!
-

PAT HARRISON

- Find players and coaches that represent the best in your sport and learn from them.

- Don't accept the status quo of your location   look beyond.
- Dream as big as you can, then do the work that will make your dream a reality.
- Create a vision for yourself—it stems from your dream. Your vision is the creative base, your building block for everything you desire to achieve.
- Look for every opportunity to challenge yourself. Being willing to challenge yourself means removing *failure* from your vocabulary and replacing it with the willingness to grow!
- Look for others whose shoulders you can stand on as you move forward on your journey.
- Listen to where your heart wants to take you—be open to the challenges and opportunities that are presented to you, wherever they might come from.
- Face your demons—we all have our own histories that hold our insecurities, the things that drag us down occasionally. Mine was a feeling of not being good enough, not being worthy to play fast-pitch softball on such a high level. Whenever your head gets in the game, try to remember that it is your heart that is really in charge. It knows what it wants on this journey you are on. Trust that you have everything you need to move out of the doubt and insecurity that may be coming from your head.

My advice for parents of young players:

- Support and trust your child's journey. Let it be their path, not yours.
- Help them find the support they require to grow both physically and mentally.
- Just listen and encourage your child when times get tough.
- Talk to them about their dream, their vision.
- Try to understand what support they need to begin to walk forward and participate in those dreams.
- Playing any sport is not about being perfect, it is about embracing each experience your child has and encouraging their love of whatever sport they are drawn to.

Peggy Kellers

When people begin to understand and appreciate softball for females, they realize the important role that the game of softball has played for girls and young women for many years.

Keep in mind that females were banned from baseball because it was thought to be "too strenuous" for women (which is questionable to say the least). So, females had no choice but to turn to softball since it was similar to the game that they were banned from. Softball pioneers paved the way for young girls today to dream of becoming a member of a softball team and perhaps someday to become a softball superstar.

For me as a female athlete, softball was an opportunity to be involved in sports from a very young age. Developing my talent and fostering my competitive drive as a young girl was a dream come true. Unfortunately, many girls my age did not have that same avenue. The idea of being part of something bigger than myself gave me an unselfish, team-first attitude. Contributing to a team effort and playing to win became an important focus.

Many of us had at one time dreamed of playing for the Brakettes; we knew that young girls who watched us compete, came to one of our clinics or heard us speak, probably had that same dream. We became very conscious of giving back for the sake of those athletes who would follow in our footsteps. Making a difference was important to us—and I hope it does for every female softball player at some time in her life!

Softball also provided me with an opportunity to realize and develop important leadership skills. Not only did these skills help me in my role with the Raybestos Brakettes but also in my future career endeavors. Because I had been considered a successful softball pioneer, the opportunities I was afforded as a female athlete and coach were unique.

Early in my career, it was instilled in me to give back to the female athletes who came after me. Being a Brakette had opened doors and created opportunities for me in so many ways. It gave me the opportunity to assist others, to provide guidance to young people, to encourage their participation in softball and hopefully succeed in the sport of softball and in life.

To attain the goal of becoming a successful softball player, girls need to realize at a young age the importance of dealing with "failure." After losing a game (or even a championship), our coaches instilled in us that those experiences should be viewed as a learning opportunity rather than a failure.

It is also imperative that young girls need to fully understand the importance of teamwork. Softball is so much more than just nine individuals playing a game. The sport is unique in that each position is individual, yet to be successful, the combined efforts of each position require teamwork.

The closest example that I can think of is that of a wholesome family experience. In that type of family, maintaining a positive family name and image is important. Working together and assuming responsibility for the various tasks that are required to make it work are key elements.

As a result, the sense of family unity that develops makes it fun to be part of a bigger effort. Having each other's back, especially when one member of the family is facing adversity, is similar to the camaraderie and teamwork one experiences in softball. While having good chemistry isn't obvious on the surface, it makes a big difference when everyone is united and supporting each other.

So, for me, my advice to young girls who dream of participating in the sport of softball is to understand the importance of being a good teammate. This, in turn, will undoubtably help you become a successful softball player and, more important, a successful person in life.

Shirley Topley, Orange Lionettes, Brakettes

Early in my career, I had tried out for a well-known Canadian softball squad, but I was immediately cut from the team. The coach told me in no uncertain terms that I would never be good enough or experienced enough to ever play softball.

I told myself from that day on that I would work hard and prove that coach wrong. So I worked hard and practiced hard. I joined other teams and played well.

Then in 1962, I was asked to join the great Orange Lionettes, and we went on to win the world championship that year. It got even better for me when I was asked to become a member of the world-famous Raybestos Brakettes. I even became the Brakettes batting champion in 1963 and 1964. All told, I played twenty-six years of amateur softball at a high level and one year of softball at a professional level when, in 1976, the Women's Professional Softball League became a reality. In addition, I coached women's softball for a total of thirty-six years.

And so, for that coach that told me years ago that I would never be good enough to play competitive softball, I say "Thank you," because that experience taught me a valuable lesson and served to strengthen my resolve to become successful in the world of women's softball.

I hope my experience serves as a teaching moment for all the young girls who are interested in fast-pitch softball. Confidence is so important in sports and also in life!

So my advice to young girls who dream of becoming a star in women's softball is to have confidence in your abilities, to work hard and to never give up on your dream.

13

LEGACY

When I grew up, we had no choice but to idolize men like Mickey Mantle.
Now girls can grow up idolizing women in team sports.
—*Joan Joyce.*

Legacy defined: "A lasting impact on the world; a gift that is passed down through generations"

The Legacy Gift Passed Down
by Fast-Pitch Softball Pioneers

The pioneers of fast-pitch softball have passed on a well-lit torch! It is important to note that today's players stand on the shoulders of all these very talented pioneers!
—*Peggy Kellers, Brakettes*

It is important to understand that in years past, while young girls were allowed to participate in individual sporting events, these same young girls could not even dream of becoming a member of a team sport. That was a dream reserved only for young boys. The softball pioneers such as those who played for the Brakettes changed that. Women softball pioneers, through their hard work and struggles, laid the groundwork for future generations.

Young girls growing up now can see themselves achieving success and fame as a member of a team sport and not just individual sporting events. Because of athletic pioneers like Joan Joyce and many others, women now have the chance for identification with a team and for work opportunities as coaches, administrators and broadcasters and endorsements after their playing careers.

The Legacy Gift Passed Down by the Brakettes and Falcons

In the history of women's softball, the Brakettes of Stratford have stood head and shoulders above all other teams—so much so that the town of Stratford, Connecticut, has been known as the "Softball Capital of the World" and the "Mecca of Women's Softball." As previously noted, the Brakettes are recognized as the greatest organized women's sports franchise of all time. This franchise has established records that will stand for quite some time. The Brakettes organization has turned out many hall of famers, Olympians and former players who have become successful softball coaches.

Likewise, the Connecticut Falcons were the most dominant team in the Women's Professional Softball League. Like the Brakettes, the Falcons (as part of the WPS) paved the way for girls and women for future generations—this time on a professional level. As tennis great and co-founder of the WPS Billie Jean King stated, "WPS is the first women's professional league and the first to be owned by women athletes. I guess we're pioneers. We're working to pave the way for girls and women in years to come."

The legacy of the Brakettes and the Falcons teams has been their ability to succeed at the highest level and thrive in fast-pitch softball as true competitors, as champions and with the common goal of always putting the team first.

But their unparalleled records and success only tell half of the story. For many former softball players, their love of the game far exceeded the individual records they achieved in their careers.

The mark of successful softball athletes (like former Brakettes and Falcons players) lies not just in the records they set but in their ability and willingness to "pay it forward." A successful women's softball athlete does not rest on her laurels but rather relishes the idea of sharing her gift, becoming a positive role model and passing on what she has learned throughout her career to young people. This is why so many former softball players (and athletes in general) become coaches, teachers and sports advocates.

From their inception, the Brakettes and Falcons ownerships have instilled in their teams' managers, coaches and players the importance of hard work, loyalty, teamwork, discipline, competitiveness, a healthy respect for their competitors, resiliency, compassion, character and a sincere respect for the game they truly love—the game of fast-pitch softball.

The success of the Brakettes and the Connecticut Falcons players on the field directly translated to their abilities to succeed in life.

And so, the legend lives on.

> *If you're going to live, leave a legacy. Make a mark on the world that can't be erased.*
> *—Maya Angelou*

Joan Joyce demonstrating how she threw her pitches to an interested young fan (Kaylee Biehl). *Courtesy of Kathy Gage.*

Inspiration. Softball player Alyssa Colangelo admires Joan Joyce sign at Waterbury's Joan Joyce Field. *Author's collection.*

Judy Martino and fan (*left*); Joan Joyce providing advice to one of her FAU players (*right*). *Courtesy of Joan Chandler.*

Clockwise from top left: Joan and her young fans (Bridget and Meghan); Margie Law of the Phoenix Ramblers; and Joan Joyce in China sharing advice with young fans. *Courtesy of IWPS website and Joan Chandler.*

Left to right: Orange Lionettes signing softballs for fans; Joan Joyce signing autographs for a group of admiring children. *Courtesy of Joan Chandler and IWPS site.*

Left to right: Joan Joyce points the way for future generation of stars; six-year-old Richard shows Joan the scrapbook he made of her career. *Courtesy of Joan Chandler.*

AFTERWORD

A must read to be "in the know" about the history of our sport, and the legendary teams like the Brakettes and the Connecticut Falcons.

As you have read in his book, Tony Renzoni pays homage to members of two legendary women's softball teams: the Brakettes and the Connecticut Falcons. Reading this book certainly has a very special significance to me. As a young fast-pitch player learning the game, I had heard all about the legendary players from both these teams, whom I looked up to and emulated.

I was even lucky enough to compete against the Brakettes just a couple years into my playing career.

What I appreciated the most about this book was its overriding theme—the impact that softball has had on young girls and women. Nowhere is this more prevalent than in my two favorite chapters, "Recollections" and "Players' Advice to Young Girls." The beauty of these two chapters is that they include thoughts and advice that are in the players' *own* words.

Connecticut's Girls of Summer: The Brakettes and the Falcons is written in a way that sports fans all across the country can relate to and find meaningful both in their careers and in their everyday lives.

This book is a must read to be "in the know" about the history of our sport, and the legendary teams like the Brakettes and the Connecticut Falcons, and also the iconic Joan Joyce!

Michele Smith, ESPN commentator, two-time Olympic gold medalist. *Courtesy of Michele Smith.*

In my fifty-year career as a softball fast-pitch athlete and now as an ESPN commentator, I have been a strong advocate of women in sports.

After reading Tony Renzoni's book and also his previous book *Connecticut Softball Legend Joan Joyce*, what stands out to me is Tony's passion and determination to bring women's sports even further into the spotlight where it belongs.

I hope you enjoyed reading this book and have found it as enlightening as I have!

—Michele Smith, two-time Olympic gold medalist, ESPN commentator

Author's note: Michele Smith has been the lead college color analyst on ESPN since 1998. She is a two-time Olympic gold medalist. In 2012, Smith became the first woman to serve as commentator for a nationally televised major league baseball game.

PRAISE FROM FANS

The Brakettes name has become truly identifiable with one of the finest sports franchises, not only nationally, but internationally as well! As a Connecticut resident it was easy to become a fan of such a successful and unprecedented sports team. What made it all the more satisfying for folks like me was that a fellow Waterburian, Joan Joyce, became one of the most talented and prolific record setters for the Brakettes and the Connecticut Falcons. Joanie, along with many of her outstanding teammates, set countless records and made the Brakettes a national (and international) success story.

—Marty Morra, former Waterburian, currently living in Florida

My brother Jay Santoli was actively involved with the Connecticut Falcons organization. Jay and I would go to some of the Falcons home games. What an amazing team! Because of Jay's association with the Falcons, I had the pleasure of meeting some of the very talented Falcon players. In fact, I still have a ball signed by every member of the Falcons team when they were part of the Women's Professional Softball League, which was over forty years ago.

As a native of Waterbury, I was especially interested in watching Joan Joyce's heroics both with the Brakettes and the Falcons, since Waterbury was also Joanie's hometown. Jay was also the Waterbury area Amateur Softball Association (ASA) commissioner and was inducted into the Connecticut ASA Hall of Fame in 1995.

—Fran Santoli, Waterbury

As a young boy growing up in New Haven in the 1950s, I was fortunate to be exposed to the world of softball. Most summer nights my grandfather, with whom we lived, would take my brother and me to softball games at either Rice Field, Blake Field or Beaver Pond Park.

I recall seeing fast-pitch, and slow-pitch at times, in the Industrial League games. At Blake, there sometimes were two or three games going on simultaneously as we watched from the outfield bleachers. Some of the players from these IL teams later played for big-name softball teams in and around Connecticut.

In the 1960s, my friends and me would occasionally drive to Stratford and watch the men's Raybestos Cardinals or the women's Raybestos Brakettes.

The Brakettes were special, with incredible pitchers and very talented all-around athletes. Regrettably, I never saw the great Joan Joyce pitch in person, but I did see "Blazing" Bertha Reagan Tickey pitch a no-hitter. Two amazing pitchers!

Fast-pitch softball was really alive in Connecticut in those days, with the women's game taking a backseat to no one!
—*Bill Rienzi, Branford*

When I was in high school, I played for the Murray Park girls softball team in Waterbury, Connecticut. Our nemesis was the softball team from the Town Plot area. Of course, we were all very familiar with the amazing Raybestos Brakettes from nearby Stratford. As a pitcher, my idol was another Waterbury girl—Joan Joyce!
—*Pat Serafin Mathews, Waterbury*

One evening, when I was a young teenager, my dad (Ernie) drove me to buy some drums in New Haven. On the way back we drove through Stratford on I-95. I looked to my right and saw a well-lit baseball field with a huge crowd in attendance. Judging from the look of the field and the large attendance, I thought for sure it was a minor league or even a major league game that was taking place. I asked my dad what that was all about. I figured he would know since he played baseball at the minor league level. He explained, "That's the Raybestos Brakettes playing, and they are the greatest women's softball team in the world. And their pitcher, Joan Joyce, is so dominant that she could strikeout most men in the major leagues!" I found out that my dad was a huge fan of the Brakettes.

Hearing my dad and getting a glimpse of that stadium really intrigued me. I didn't realize that a women's softball team which was so famous came from my home state of Connecticut. Well, I certainly do now. That image of seeing the Brakettes field with that enormous crowd has stayed with me ever since.

We in Connecticut are very proud of the historic contributions and the significance of the Brakettes to the softball world and, overall, to women's sports.
—*Ken Evans, Stamford and member of the successful Fifth Estate Band*

INTERVIEWS

Interview with Kristine Botto Drust, Brakettes Assistant Coach, October 25, 2022

[Coaching the Brakettes] is a dream opportunity. For me, it's the best time ever!
—*Kristine Botto Drust*

TR First of all, congratulations on your wonderful career as a player and as an assistant coach.

KBD   Thank you very much Tony.

TR Where were you born and raised?

KBD   I was born and raised in Lowell, Massachusetts.

TR What schools did you attend?

KBD   I attended St. Louis Elementary School, Lowell High School and UMass Lowell.

TR When you were in elementary school, did you play any sports?

KBD   Yep, at St. Louis Elementary I played softball, soccer and was a cheerleader for the boys' basketball team.

TR Were you allowed to play baseball in Little League?

KBD   Yes, girls were allowed to play baseball. I did play T-ball. I was definitely a beneficiary of Title IX. But my heart was in playing softball, and my parents realized this.

Kristine Botto Drust with a leaping catch. *Courtesy of Allan MacTaggart.*

TR What sports did you play in high school?

KBD In high school, I was the goalie on the soccer varsity team; I ran track and played softball.

TR What sports did you play in college?

KBD In college, I played softball, played a little soccer as a goalie and I threw shotput on the track team.

TR Did you have any sports idols when you were growing up?

KBD I have to say that my sports idols growing up were my two older brothers (Steve and Mike), who played baseball, soccer and basketball at a high level.

TR What was your major at UMass Lowell?

KBD I had a double major in criminal justice and psychology.

TR How did you become interested in sports?

KBD My dad (Stephen) played softball, and I grew up around the world of sports, especially watching my two brothers play baseball. They let me use their gloves when I started to play baseball and softball. And my sister (Keri) played a little sports and was a cheerleader. My mom (Colleen) didn't have many sports opportunities as a female growing up at that time, but she did run track. She said I got my speed from her. She was very fast and would actually outrun the boys in the schoolyard. It was kind of like the rite of passage for me to become interested in sports, particularly softball [*laughter*].

TR When was the first time you played organized softball?

KBD When I was fifteen years old, I played for the Dracut Crush women's softball team.

TR The Dracut Crush? Sounds like a tough team!

KBD [*Laughter*] We were!

TR Did you receive support from your parents to participate in sports?

KBD I was lucky. I got the best kind of support from my parents. They were very supportive of my coaches and never bad-mouthed or second-guessed the coaches or players. When I got in the car after a game, the first thing they would ask me was did I have fun. They would always tell me that "you did your best and that is all you can ask for." They offered a ton of respect for everyone around me and my teammates.

TR Growing up, did you have any hobbies outside of softball?

KBD I loved being outside, playing kickball and all the school yard games we played.

TR Aside from the Dracut Crush, what other teams did you play softball on?

KBD After the Dracut Crush, I played for the Haverhill Hurricanes softball team, the Bay State Bullets (an under-eighteen softball team), and also played sports on my college teams. After college, I played three seasons for the Connecticut Classics women's softball team from 2001 to 2003.

In 2004, I got a call from John Stratton to play for the Brakettes. Because I had hurt my knees playing sports in college, playing the outfield (as opposed to catching or another position) made the most sense. At that time, I was traveling from Lowell, Massachusetts, to Stratford to play with the Brakettes.

Knowing about my long commute, Johnny called me at the end of April 2005 to inform me that I had the opportunity to play in my hometown of Lowell for the National Professional Fast-Pitch Softball (NPF) team called the New England Riptide. The owner of the Riptide had called John to ask if I would be willing to play for his team. And so, on May 21, 2005 (my twenty-sixth birthday), I joined the Riptide. The home field was actually in Lowell, so that worked out well for me.

I played for the New England Riptide for two seasons (2005–6) as a utility player. In 2006, our Riptide team beat the Brakettes for the 2006 NPF Championship. Actually, the night before the championship game my now husband (Don) proposed to me. And so, with winning the 2006 NPF Championship and with banged up knees, I thought it was a very good way to end my career in front of my family and friends, playing for my hometown New England Riptide team.

TR You were inducted into the Connecticut Softball Hall of Fame in 2018. Were you inducted into any other halls of fame?

KBD I was honored to also be inducted into the Lowell High School Hall of Fame and the UMass Lowell Hall of Fame.

TR Tell me what it is like to coach with John Stratton as the team manager.

KBD I have had the pleasure and honor of working under Johnny as the Brakettes assistant coach since 2015. As you know, Johnny has been associated with the Brakettes organization for over seventy-five years and his amazing legacy speaks for itself.

Johnny is small on words but high on love. He truly just coaches through love. He puts trust in players that he single-handedly selected to come represent our program. His presence, his pursuit of excellence and his knowledge hold us all accountable to get better every single day. So he is all about trust, love and accountability.

For John, it's never really about words during pregame, during the game or post game. His coaching is watching how well players are performing in their colleges and how well they represent their school's program. He puts his trust in the preparation and the selection of these athletes. Do they have the fundamentals and the level of skills needed to be a Brakette? And once he invites them to join the team, he just puts his trust and his love in the athlete.

Johnny always keeps things simple. He trusts that you are the player to apply what he says and then go out and become a successful player. He earns the highest level of respect you can give a coach from his players.

When you play for or coach with John Stratton you come to realize that he represents not only his current team members but also all the women who have played for the Brakettes since 1947.

John Stratton is totally committed to preserving the Brakettes legacy.

TR How would you sum up your experience as a coach of the Brakettes?

KBD I am deeply grateful to be given the dream opportunity of becoming a part of such a legendary sports organization, to work under an amazing manager, to be able to coach so many outstanding athletes. I treasure the fun times we have, the commitment to excellence which we all share and just being around all these very talented and wonderful players. For me, it's the best time ever!

INTERVIEW WITH JOAN JOYCE

Author's note: The legendary Joan Joyce passed away on March 26, 2022. Because of the intense interest in Joan's career and life, I would like to repeat a 2018 interview I had with Joanie that appears in my previous book *Connecticut Softball Legend Joan Joyce*. I hope you find this interview as interesting and enjoyable as I did. Joanie, you are dearly missed!

> *July 2, 2018*
> *In all honesty, I would have hated to hit against me. You almost had to guess what I would be throwing. And you had to be ready to swing when you immediately saw the ball leaving my hand.* [Joan snaps her fingers] *That is how much time the batter had to swing at my pitch.*
> *Otherwise, you weren't going to hit it.*
> —*Joan Joyce*

TR Joanie, thank you for agreeing to this interview.

JJ My pleasure, Tony.

TR Is it alright with you if I refer to you as Joanie?

JJ Absolutely! I tell everyone down here in Florida that I am best known in Connecticut as Joanie Joyce. Down here, I'm known as Joan.

TR First of all, I wanted to congratulate you on your outstanding career. I also wanted to congratulate you on your upcoming induction into the Atlantic Sun Hall of Fame in August 2018.

JJ Thank you very much. The Division 1 Atlantic Sun conference (originally known as the Trans America Athletic conference) was the very first conference that my softball team at Florida Atlantic University played in. We dominated that conference. Then we went from there to the Division 1 Sun Belt, and then from the Sun Belt we went to Division 1 Conference USA.

Joan Joyce was a one-of-a-kind multidimensional athlete, starring in numerous sports. *Courtesy of Jim Fetter and Joan Chandler.*

TR We have a couple of things in common. Like you, I was born and raised in Waterbury, Connecticut. I lived in the Town Plot section. I played baseball and basketball on fields and parks that you mentioned in previous interviews, Fulton Park, City Mills, Town Plot Park, etc. Of course, I certainly didn't play ball on the level that you played. I guess one of my "claims to fame" was that Terry Tata umpired our games. He then went on to have a great career as a major league umpire. Also, growing up I was a big admirer of Mickey Mantle, who was your idol growing up in Waterbury.

JJ I went to school with Terry Tata at Crosby. He lived right down the street from me in Waterbury. I knew Terry well. Great guy. And I have a photo of Mickey Mantle in my office. I had the pleasure of playing golf with Mickey.

TR I saw the video of the renaming of a facility next to Waterbury's Municipal Stadium in your name. That was really cool.

JJ Yes, it was. Municipal Stadium has two parts to it. They have the baseball field, and they have a softball field right next to it. That is the field that they named for me. It's a very nice field, and it was an honor.

TR OK, I'd like to ask you a few questions about growing up in Waterbury, Connecticut. First of all, where did you live in Waterbury?

JJ I first lived on Hill Street, and then when I was around eight years old my family moved to Tudor Street in Waterbury. As I mentioned, Terry Tata lived down the street from me. And when I was in eighth grade, I actually helped a fellow build a house, about three or four houses up the street. For a time growing up, I wanted to be a carpenter. I was walking by, and a guy was building this house. And, of course, nosey me asked the fellow if he needed help. So it ended up that it was this seventy-five-year-old carpenter and myself who built the house. [*Laughter*] I did everything. I put roofs on, I put tiles in the bathrooms, everything. And so, my parents ended up buying the house that the guy and I built. For helping to build the house, the contractor (Tommy Garafola) bought me a beautiful bicycle, which I loved. I would ride my bike around the neighborhood. As you know, Waterbury has these steep hills, so I had to stay on the flat streets around my house. So that's where I lived in Waterbury. Hill Street when I was really little and then Tudor Street.

TR Where did your mom and dad work in Waterbury?

JJ My dad, Joe, was a foreman at Scovill's factory. My mom (Jean) worked at Chase Brass & Copper Company. Actually, they worked different shifts so that one of my parents would be home to watch us kids. My father would work either the 11:00 p.m.–7:00 a.m. shift or 7:00 a.m.–3:00 p.m. He mainly worked the 11:00 p.m.–7:00 a.m. I remember him coming home in the morning bringing us donuts for breakfast. And then after taking us to school, he would take my mother to work at 3:00 p.m. and then he would take my brother, Joe Jr., and me to the ballfield or basketball court. My sister, Janis, stayed home.

TR I'm interested in your father playing both fast-pitch softball and basketball. Who did he play for and where did he play?

JJ My father played for everyone! [*Laughter.*] But he mainly played for the Waterbury Bombers down at Waterbury's City Mills park. He played with guys like Tony Marinaro, Ike Icovone, Joe Byne and Dick Ierardi. They were all great! My father played third base for the Waterbury Bombers.

TR I remember watching them play. They were great, an exciting team to watch.

JJ Yep, they sure were. They were probably one notch below the Raybestos Cardinals, who were our men's team at Raybestos. They would be competitive against the Cardinals, but the Cardinals would end up winning, mainly because of the Cardinals' pitching. Tony Marinaro of the Waterbury Bombers was our mailman. In the summertime, I used to go up to the top of the hill to help him deliver. [*Laughter*] In return, he would spend about twenty minutes with me to teach me softball. Tony Marinara actually was the one that told me about the Raybestos Brakettes.

TR What team did your father play basketball for?

JJ   My dad played for a number of basketball teams. He played for Crosby High School, Waterbury Knights of Lithuania, Scovill's and the New Britain Cremos. In the winter, we would be going to games just about every night. I remember that whenever there was a time out or at half time, my brother Joe and I would immediately run out on the gym floor to make sure to be first to grab a basketball and shoot.

TR   Did your parents go to your games?

JJ   Oh yeah, they made a point to attend all my games. The only exception was golf. They didn't understand that game. One time my mother did go to one of my golf matches. My mother was sitting in a chair off the tenth green. After I finished putting, my mother said to me, "Joanie, I'll wait here until you get back." I told her, "Mom, I won't be back here until tomorrow!" [*Laughter*] My biggest fan was my dad (Joe Sr.). He would closely observe me whether I was pitching or hitting. Afterward he would offer his advice. If I went three for four, a family member would ask, "Why didn't you go four for four?" [*Laughter*] Both my parents were very, very supportive! Up until his death in 2013, my father made a point to attend all my softball games, as a player and as a coach.

TR   What schools did you attend in Waterbury?

JJ   I attended Webster Grammar School, graduating in the spring of 1954. I then attended Crosby High School in September 1954 and graduated in the spring of 1958. Webster and Crosby High Schools are in Waterbury.

TR   Tell me about your experience with the Little League.

JJ   When I was twelve years old, my brother would take me down to City Mills where his Little League team played. So, I got to practice a lot with the boys on the Little League team. When the league began, I remember going up to a Little League stadium up on Watertown Avenue. So I played a game with the boys' Little League team. I was their catcher.

TR   How did you do playing on their team?

JJ   I knocked a couple of balls off the fence. I got a triple and a double in the game.

TR   Really?

JJ   Yep. But after the game, I was told by the administrator, "Girls are not allowed to play in Little League." I'm sure it was because I knocked some balls over the outfielders' heads. [*Laughter*] They just didn't want me to show up the boys in the league.

TR So you were kicked off the team after that one game?

JJ Right.

TR After playing the one game with the Little Leaguers and getting kicked out, did you play softball at age twelve?

JJ Oh sure. I used to play softball at Fulton Park. In the summer, they would have a tournament with teams from all the parks in Waterbury. So our team (Fulton Park) would play against all the other teams from Waterbury Parks. The person who was our "coach" really didn't know anything about softball. So, I ended up being our coach! [*Laughter*]

TR Did you pitch when you played for Fulton Park?

JJ Yes, that is where I first started to pitch. But it was the type of pitching where you would let all the kids hit. But still I got to pitch and play the field a lot.

TR So, when did you begin with the Raybestos Brakettes?

JJ At age thirteen, right after playing for Fulton Park.

TR At age thirteen?

JJ Yep. I tried out for the Raybestos Brakettes at age thirteen, and I made the team.

TR When did you learn to use the "slingshot" method of pitching?

JJ When I was sixteen, a pitcher by the name of John "Cannonball" Baker happened to be up on a ladder, putting up bunting for a Raybestos game. Cannonball pitched against the Raybestos Cardinals. At one point, he looked down and saw me pitching, using the "windmill" delivery, which is a very common pitching method. So, Cannonball yells down to me, "Hey, why don't you use the slingshot delivery?" I told him I was not familiar with that delivery. So he came down from the ladder and began to show me the "slingshot." He encouraged me to use that method since I would be able to generate a lot more speed, power and accuracy using that delivery. I had been pitching for a year or two before that. But I was wild and would actually hit batters. I hated it. So, I began practicing the slingshot for twenty to thirty minutes, until I got comfortable. It didn't take long for me to adapt to that delivery method. As soon as I changed to the "slingshot," it was a totally different world. A totally different scene! That one year, it was unbelievable the difference in my pitching.

TR So once he showed you how to use the slingshot delivery, how long did it take you to use that delivery method in a game?

JJ   I used it immediately! And what a difference it made. I was now able to pitch the ball with total accuracy, and I was able to generate a lot more power using the slingshot. Such a great feeling to be in total control of all my pitches.

TR   Sounds like "destiny" to me. I mean, what are the chances of someone like that being up there at that very moment—who was not associated with your team or even the men's Raybestos team—showing you an entirely different delivery method which would alter your pitching career forever?

JJ   Yes, it was definitely fate or destiny, or whatever you want to call it. These "destiny" things happened to me all my life! I guess part of it is being in the right place at the right time.

TR   Yep, but it's also acting on your gut feelings and working hard to perfect these suggestions, which obviously you did.

JJ   Yes, that's true.

TR   Did you get a chance to thank Cannonball?

JJ   Oh yeah, certainly.

TR   That must have been a turning point for you.

JJ   A major turning point!

TR   In 1956, Bertha Ragan joined the Brakettes after being the star pitcher for California's Orange Lionettes. What impact did Bertha Ragan have on the Brakettes?

JJ   It was a major impact. When Bertha joined the team, she changed the whole complexion of the team. She was so good. She changed everything not by words but by her actions. We began to really believe in ourselves, and our team became very competitive. Bertha led by example. I was only fifteen years old, and my pitching delivery was completely different than Bertha's delivery. She was a figure-eight pitcher, so it was difficult for us to relate to each other from a pitching standpoint. But I was certainly influenced by Bertha's winning attitude.

TR   As a teenager what type of music and recording artists did you listen to?

JJ   I was at the age of watching Elvis come on the scene. But you know what? My absolute favorites were Johnny Mathis and Bobby Vinton. I think I still have every one of their albums, and I still play their songs. "Chances Are," by Jonny Mathis, such a wonderful song!

TR   So you graduated from Crosby High School in 1958. Did you go to school after that?

JJ Yes, I attended Southern Connecticut State College but left after a year because I wanted to get a job. So I worked at Raybestos for about a year. Then I worked at Lakewood Lanes bowling alley in Waterbury for about six months. All the while, I was officiating girls' basketball. The day after I officiated a game between Waterbury Catholic High School and Stamford Catholic High, I got a call and was offered a job coaching the WCHS girls' basketball team for the 1960 season. The following year, 1961, I became the phys ed teacher and coach of the girls' basketball and volleyball team at WCHS. I did this at WCHS from 1961 to 1963. In 1963, I decided I wanted to go away for a while but at the same time pursue my college and softball careers. I thought to myself, where can I go that would have a softball team that was almost as successful as the Brakettes? That's when I decided to join the powerhouse Orange Lionettes and attend Chapman College, which were both located in Orange, California. This was in September 1963.

TR When did you return to Connecticut?

JJ I graduated from Chapman in the spring of 1966. I then returned to Connecticut after my 1966 season with the Lionettes.

TR Did you face Ted Williams other than your encounters at Waterbury's Municipal Stadium?

JJ I actually faced Ted Williams several times. The first time I pitched to Ted was at his camp in Lakeville, Massachusetts. This was in May 1961. I had a sore shoulder when I faced him in Lakeville so I didn't want to throw hard and allowed all the batters to hit, including Ted. At the camp, Ted mentioned that he was asked by some promoters to bat against me in August at Municipal Stadium in Waterbury. So I faced him again in August 1961. Actually, I pitched to Ted several times, the event in Massachusetts and several times in Waterbury. Our last matchup was in 1966.

TR Jumping ahead in your softball career, what was the "Joan Joyce Rule"?

JJ That was when I pitched for the Connecticut Falcons. The Falcons were part of the Women's Professional League (WPS). The WPS league organizers said I was too dominant against other teams so they decided to move the pitcher's mound back four feet, from forty feet to forty-four feet. The reason they gave was that by moving the mound back four feet, it would make it a bit easier to hit against me. They called it the "Joan Joyce Rule." So I had to relearn how to pitch, and I made the adjustment to the point where I became comfortable pitching at that distance.

TR I would say so, because I know there were games right after they moved the mound in which you pitched some great games. Which batter was the toughest for you to get out?

JJ Carol Spanks. She had a good batting eye. In my opinion, she was one of the best hitters in the game. I actually developed a special screwball pitch just for her (down and in) to get her out.

TR In the very first game of the 1976 WPS World Series, you pitched against the San Jose Sunbirds. The Falcons won the game 3–0. Charlotte Graham was the pitcher for the Sunbirds. What do you remember about that first game?

JJ The first game was held at Meriden's Falcon Field. Going into the championship, I was 39-2 in the regular season. Charlotte and the Sunbirds were very good, but we were confident about our chances of winning, especially after having done well in the playoffs. The one thing I remember about Charlotte is that she dug a hole in front of the pitcher's mound so deep that I was afraid I would break my ankle if I stepped into it. [*Laughter*]

TR In 1979, the Falcons traveled to China on a goodwill tour, playing softball and participating in clinics. What was the experience of playing in China like?

JJ It was a phenomenal experience! I was told that the Connecticut Falcons were the first organized team to play in mainland China. We played in front of massive crowds. *People* magazine sent a reporter there to cover our experience in China. They had cameras on me everywhere and filmed all of my pitching deliveries. They actually asked me to go back to China for six months and teach them more about pitching, but I said no. I think I would have really starved because I could not adapt to the food there. I mean I was on chocolate the entire time there! [*Laughter*] My room overlooked the street, and every morning a truck would pull up and the driver would toss meat at the entrance to the place we were staying in, pigs and whatnot, and someone would drag the meat into the kitchen. So that was the end of me eating the food there. I stuck with my chocolate bars! [*Laughter*] I brought my golf club with the hope of practicing my golf game while I was there. Boy, was I surprised because there was no grass there! Actually, I was hoping to drive a golf ball over the Great Wall of China but I forgot to bring my club. And, anyway, I'm not sure the authorities would have let me do that! [*Laughter*] But, overall, it was such a one-time phenomenal experience!

TR You had so many no-hitters and amazing games as a pitcher. What was your worst game as pitcher?

JJ   I would have to say it was a game in Buffalo, when I pitched for the Falcons. We were playing the Buffalo Breskis that night. I remember that it was a beautiful day in Buffalo. It was so warm that I didn't even bring my jacket to the game. About an hour before game time, the weather changed dramatically. The temperature dropped at least thirty degrees, with the wind blowing very strong. We suddenly experienced the wind effect coming off the lake in the Buffalo area. We went from short sleeves to being freezing. The wind gusts were blowing from home plate to center field. Pop ups were blowing out of the park. I know because I popped a ball up myself and it flew out of the ballpark for a home run. [*Laughter*] I asked our coach Brenda (Reilly) to take me out of the game. Brenda replied, "No, I think it would be good for you to experience one game in your life in which you knew what it was like to get your butt kicked!" [*Laughter*]

TR Let's say it's tie score, bases loaded, last inning, two outs and the count is 3-2, which pitch would you throw?

JJ   Depends.

TR Would it depend on whether it was a right-handed or left-handed hitter or the type of hitter?

JJ   The type of hitter. For example, Shirley Topley, who was a very good player, could hit my rise ball but not my drop. So if I needed a strikeout, Shirley would get nothing but drops.

TR But did you have a "go to" pitch in key situations?

JJ   No. I trusted both my rise ball and drop ball enough to throw in any situations. I threw hard enough that either the rise ball or drop ball would not only reach the plate fast but would move dramatically. In all honesty, I would have hated to hit against me. You almost had to guess what I would be throwing. And you had to be ready to swing when you immediately saw the ball leaving my hand. Otherwise, you weren't going to hit it. [Joan snaps her fingers.] That's how fast the pitch is and how much time you had to swing!

TR How fast did you throw?

JJ   I have no idea. And, of course, there were no radar guns in those days. I'm told the pitches were 119 miles per hour, in terms of reaction time. When I was pitching in California, there was this gal (Fran Shaftma) who did her doctorate at USC on softball pitching. She brought all of the top pitchers in from the Pacific Coast League, and she put us through different tests for three days at Long Beach State College. In that study, it showed that my pitches were coming into the batter with a reaction time of a pitch coming in at 119 miles per hour.

TR You once said in a newspaper interview that you were so competitive that if your mother or father wanted to bat against you, that you would have to strike them out. If your dad did step up to the plate, what pitch would you throw him to strike him out?

JJ [*Laughter*] Well, I'll tell you, I actually did pitch to my dad once. He came home from work one day and started needling me, saying, "I can hit you." I told him, "Oh no you can't." So he gets his bat and says, "Ok, let's see what you got." So I throw him a rise ball. On the first pitch, my dad fouls the ball off, and it goes right through our house window. My mother wanted to kill us! [*Laughter*] So that was the only time I threw a pitch to my father. We didn't want any more broken windows! [*Laughter*]

TR Ok, so what pitch would you throw to your mother?

JJ Oh, that wouldn't even be a contest! A very slow ball, I guess. [*Laughter*] I think the only sport my mother played was bowling. She liked that.

TR Did you play softball during the winter?

JJ I never threw once during the wintertime. After the softball season ended, it was time to concentrate on other winter sports like basketball, volleyball, even bowling. I don't know that I would have liked playing one sport all year long. I would have been bored to death.

TR Let's turn to basketball. Did you play basketball in school?

JJ Yes. When I was a freshman at Crosby High, I played intermural basketball. We actually played a six-player game. One day, I saw in the newspaper that there were tryouts for the Libra AA Women's Basketball team in Waterbury. So I asked my father if I could try out. He said he would take me there, but he would have to see what it's all about. I was only fifteen at the time. So I tried out and I made the team. I played with Libra AA for about a year. When I was a junior at Crosby High I tried out and made the New London Wheels women's basketball team in New London, Connecticut. It was a very good team. They asked me to play in a national tournament. I believe I was sixteen at this time. I know I didn't have my license yet. A friend of mine from Hamden also was on the New London Wheels. So she would have to pick me up and drive to the games. We competed in several national championships of the Women's Basketball Association (WBA). For women at the time, the six-player basketball game was always used. The WBA was unique because it was a five-player game, a precursor of how the game would be played in years to come.

TR What position did you play in basketball?

JJ I played forward.

TR It sounds to me that you really liked basketball.

JJ Oh yeah, that was my favorite—by far. I loved playing basketball. My dad told me all the time that I was better in basketball than softball.

TR Wow! That's saying a lot!

TR When did you take up bowling?

JJ I bowled right along, during the whole time. In the wintertime, I bowled in numerous leagues. Friday nights "pots" down in Ansonia, where we bowled for money. I remember when I was a student at New Haven's Southern Connecticut State College, going to Ansonia and bowled pretty much all night. We didn't start bowling until 11:00 p.m. or midnight. Actually, that was big-time stuff. I remember bowling in some very big money leagues.

TR I heard that you once bowled against a very popular singer. What's the story behind that?

JJ I was working at Raybestos at the time. My father read about a new ten-pin bowling alley in Waterbury, I think it was Lakewood Lanes. This was in 1960. So, my brother, Joe, my father and myself decided to bowl there. At 5:30 p.m., there were cars all over the place and a large crowd to get into the bowling lanes. I went to go in and make reservations for us to bowl later. However, a policeman stopped me and said I could not go in because it's the grand opening at the bowling lanes and they were having a big private party. The officer said they would be open to the public at 8:30 p.m. Then, somebody spots me, brings me inside and has me meet all these people, including the owners of the bowling alleys, who were from Massachusetts. One of the owners suggested that they put on a contest between myself and the special party guest singer Brian Hyland. Brian had a No. 1 Billboard hit in 1960 with his song "Itsy Bitsy Teenie Weenie Yellow Polka Dot Bikini." So he was extremely popular at the time. But I told the owners no, because I was a duckpin bowler and only bowled ten-pin bowling once in my life. But they insisted. I told them OK, but first I had to pick up my father and brother, and I would be back. So now here I am in a ten-pin contest with Brian Hyland. Like I said, I only bowled with ten-pin once, so I had to figure out how to bowl properly. Anyway, I bowl 130 and he bowls 99. The owners said give him another chance and bowl another game. So we bowl another game. This time, I bowl 199 and I trounced him! [*Laughter*] Brian is a great guy! After we were done, the owners call me into the office and offer me a job to become a professional bowler. My job was to bowl twenty games a day and I would get paid for it. At the time I was a basketball official, so after the basketball game I would go to the bowling alley at night until 2:00 a.m. or 3:00 a.m. Now, the wife of the manager of the bowling alley happened to be the best bowler in Waterbury. However, soon after I started bowling ten-pin, my bowling average topped hers. So now she is not too happy about this. [*Laughter*] And then she started putting all these restrictions on me and made it miserable. Finally, I told the manager I can't do this any longer. So I left. [*Laughter*.]

TR How did you get involved in volleyball?

JJ I left Orange, California, and returned to Connecticut in September 1966. In October, I attended the National Association of Girls and Women in Sport (NAGWS) in Indiana. I was delighted to find out that Hall of Famer Patsy Neal was in charge of NAGWS. It was there that I learned "power volleyball." Returning from the NAGWS clinic, I was recruited to play for a team in New Jersey. So I brought Donna Lopiano and Brenda Reilly down with me to play on the team. At that time, I was also the player/coach for the Raybestos Brakettes basketball team. Our basketball team was pretty good, Donna Lopiano and people like that. We played in a league that was all over New England. We would have to drive all the way up to New Hampshire to play basketball. And we would slaughter everybody! I mean, we would beat everyone by thirty or forty points! [*Laughter*] And then we would go to the national tournament. But we would get beat because we would play against all the big teams, like the very strong Tennessee National Business College team. We just never played at that level of competition. Raybestos didn't want to sponsor the basketball team to that level because it would cost a lot more money. So then I decided this isn't fun, going all the way up to New Hampshire and beating teams by thirty or forty points. So then I said, why don't we try volleyball. We started by playing all over in the USVBA— in Connecticut, New Jersey, New York, Pennsylvania, Ohio, Canada. We played in some national tournaments. We drove all over the place. We would drive to Ohio on Friday, for instance, and play until three or four in the morning, sleep for a few hours, play volleyball all day on Saturday and then have to drive home on Sunday. Most of the kids who played were teachers. So we had to get back by Sunday night to get to the schools for Monday morning. So we did that for a few years. And so I decided to start my own volleyball team and called them the Connecticut Clippers.

TR Tell me about your experience with the *Superstars Competition*.

JJ I was in the *Superstars Competition* on ABC TV in 1975 and 1979. They wouldn't let me get into the softball throw or golf because you couldn't participate in any event that you were a "star" in. And volleyball was out. So softball, golf and volleyball were events that I had a chance to win, but I wasn't eligible. Wonderful to compete with so many great athletes.

TR Tell me about being inducted into the Connecticut Women's Hall of Fame.

JJ It was an unbelievable hall of fame! I was impressed and honored being inducted into the Connecticut Women's Hall of Fame.

TR Since you were not a paid athlete for most of your career, where did you work when you returned to Connecticut in 1966?

JJ I was a teacher and coach at Presentation High School (Stamford), St. Mary's High School (Greenwich), Bethel High School, Brooklyn (NY) College and Mattatuck Community College in Waterbury.

TR What sports did you coach at these schools?

JJ I was the coach of the basketball, volleyball and, in the case of Brooklyn and Mattatuck Colleges, the girls' softball teams.

TR I also read that you owned your own travel agency. Is that true?

JJ I was employed as a part-time travel consultant at Paradise Travel in the mid-1960s. Later, I started my own travel agency (Joan Joyce All-Star Travel Agency), renting space in the Trumbull Shopping Plaza. My sister, Janis, ran the agency.

TR Joyce Compton, your teammate with the Brakettes and Falcons, also worked at Mattatuck College, is that right?

JJ Here's what happened there. When I was at Brooklyn College, I saw an ad for a coaching position at Mattatuck College in my hometown of Waterbury. I called, and I spoke with John Salerno, who was the athletic director and men's basketball coach at the college. John informed me that there was an opening for a coach, but it was a part-time position. I told John that I couldn't take the job because I needed full-time employment like I had in Brooklyn. John called me back and said he spoke with the college president, and they decided to make it a full-time job and offered me the position. So I ended up being the women's athletic director and coach of the softball, basketball and volleyball teams at Mattatuck College. Toward the beginning of 1975, I figured the time was right to pursue a new challenge—golf. So I told John and the Mattatuck president that this was a challenge I felt I must pursue. I made plans to go down to Florida and start taking golf lessons. But I didn't want to leave John hanging with no coach for the women's teams. So I asked Joyce Compton if she was interested in taking my place, and she said she was very interested. Joyce was a great athlete, so I knew she would fit in fine at Mattatuck. So that is how that happened.

TR How old were you when you first took up golf on a serious basis?

JJ I took my first golf lessons a few months after my thirty-fifth birthday. I worked at golf very hard. I joined the LPGA tour when I was thirty-seven years old.

TR I heard you hit the ball very long. Do you recall how long your drive was?

JJ No, I don't remember that. I only know that Jane Blalock said I hit the ball longer than anyone else on the tour at the time. So if Jane said that, it must be true. I was told that by others also. The official who marked the courses once told me that she actually had to change the markers on the course because of the length of my drives. So I guess they were pretty long. I was also told by many people that I changed women's golf to a certain extent because I caused other girls to have to hit their golf balls longer in order to compete.

TR On May 16, 1982, you broke the LPGA (and PGA) record of the least number of putts in a single round of golf. You beat Beverly Klass's record of nineteen putts by needing only seventeen putts. Tell me about that.

JJ That was unbelievable. I chipped it in four times, one-putt eleven times and two-putt the other three greens. After the fourteenth hole, I told one of the officials that I was going to break the record. She turned to me and said, "You must be crazy!" So, I told her, well maybe, but I am going to break the record. I just knew it! [*Laughter*]

TR I should note that Beverly Klass began her golfing career at age six, whereas you began taking golf lessons at age thirty-five.

JJ Yes, I did begin my golf career a bit late. [*Laughter*]

TR John Stratton told me that you were also great at ping-pong. Is that true?

JJ [*Laughter*] I adapted to that game pretty well. One time when we were on the road, several of my FAU players started needling me and said they can beat me at ping-pong. My assistant coach Chan (Walker) challenged me to a game of ping-pong at the Tampa hotel where the team was staying. I told Chan, "You don't want to do that!" But she kept needling me saying she can beat me. So we played, and I beat her the first game. Chan tells me,

"You got lucky. Let's play another game." So I beat her the second game. I tell Chan, "What, did I get lucky again?" [*Laughter*]

TR When you were playing sports such as softball or basketball, what goals did you set for yourself?

JJ I never set any goals when I was playing. I know people set goals and stuff and it may work for them, but I never set a goal in my life. I never sat down and said this is going to be my goal for the year, I never did that. It was one pitch at a time or one shot at a time, and whatever that produced at the end of the game is what it was. I spent my whole life doing that, just one pitch at a time or one shot at a time, and it turned out pretty good.

TR Do you think that coaches today run the risk of "over-coaching" their players?

JJ Depends on the coach. I personally have witnessed coaches who would yell out instructions to each player during the game on everything the player was doing on the field. That's not allowing the kids to think for themselves, and they don't learn the intangibles of the game. For me, it all goes back to my experiences at Waterbury's City Mills park, learning for myself, and learning the instincts necessary to be a good ballplayer, things like knowing when to run to third base on a base hit to the outfield.

TR I heard that you provide sports training to your nieces and nephews?

JJ That's right. My brother, Joe, and his wife, Ginny, have five grandchildren (Morgan, Joey, Brooke, Patrick and Teagan). Whenever I visit Joe and Ginny I have the four kids stop over Joe's house for sports "camp." So what I do is take each child separately and concentrate on the sport that they are most familiar with. I then take them as a group and give training tips on sports such as basketball, lacrosse, etc. I should also mention the other grandchild, three-year-old Teagan, who is a real "spit-fire." I am blessed to have such wonderful nieces and nephews who always take advice from their Aunt Joan.

TR What advice would you give to a preteen girl who would like to be the next Joan Joyce?

JJ I would advise the young girl to play a variety of sports, love those sports and work really hard on those sports. Besides softball, the child should be involved in other sports such as basketball, volleyball, soccer, until at least she is out of high school. Be an all-around athlete. But, be a kid. Have fun. And you got to love every sport you are involved in. Learn by doing but don't involve yourself in only one sport twelve months out of the year.

TR You have been compared to the great Babe Didrikson Zaharias by many sports experts, the media and fans as the Greatest Female Athlete in Sports History. How do you feel about that?

JJ No question that Babe was a great athlete. And she played a variety of sports as I did. However, in talking to people who knew Babe and in reading about her, my understanding is that Babe was not a very well-liked individual. I have spent my entire adult life not only striving to be a great all-around athlete, but to be a good teammate, teacher and coach.

TR I have often wondered how it is that you had this amazing ability to perform so well in high-pressure situations in all sports that you were involved in (softball, golf, etc.). I discussed this with Debbie Chin, a talented athlete herself, who had an athletic career at the University of New Haven for over forty years and is your close friend. Debbie calls this ability of yours an "innate sports ability."

JJ If Debbie calls it that I would certainly believe what she said. I know that throughout my playing and coaching career (even to this day) I have always welcomed a challenge. I always wanted to be challenged and welcomed pressure situations. For whatever reasons, I was always able to remain calm in these pressure situations. I guess it is similar to Mariano Rivera coming into a game with the bases loaded and no outs or John Havlicek wanting the ball in a tie game with five seconds left.

TR How would you sum up your amazing sixty-five-year career in sports?

JJ Fun. I mean, how many people can say they have gone through their entire life having fun in what they were doing? I'll let all my accomplishments speak for themselves. But to me, I loved every sport I was involved in and whether it was as a player, a referee or a coach it has all been fun.

TR How would you like to be known in history books—your role in the history of sports?

JJ A great all-around athlete, a dominant pitcher, a great teammate, an effective teacher and a successful coach.

TR I really hope that people who read this book come away with the same conclusion as I have had for many years. In my opinion, you are the Greatest Female Athlete in Sports History and it has been my honor to tell your story.

JJ Thank you, Tony, I can't tell you how much this all means to me!

Appendix C

CONNECTICUT ASA (USA SOFTBALL) HALL OF FAME INDUCTEES

Brakettes who have been inducted into the Connecticut Softball Hall of Fame are as follows: Rosemary "Micki" Stratton (1972), Bertha Ragan Tickey (1973), Edna Fraser (1975), Ann DeLuca (1976), Kathryn "Sis" King (1976), Carol LaRose (1977), Marie Ottaviano (1979), Barbara Abernethy (1980), Beverly Mulonet (1980), Millie Elias (1982), Lorraine Meehan (1982), Peggy Kellers (1982), Willie Roze (1982), Joan Joyce (1983), Donna Lopiano (1983), Ann Edmundson (1983), Alice Dynia (1986), Mary Primavera (1986), Allyson Rioux (1989), Diane Schumacher (1992), Marjorie Gabrielle (1993), Gladys Crespo (1994), Mary Jane Hagan (1995), Barbara Reinalda (1999), Catherine Oslavsky (2004), Doreen Denmon (2005), Pat Dufficy (2006), Elaine Biercevicz Piazza (2006), Mary Schneider (2011), Patti Fernandez (2016), Amber Radomski (2017), Kristine Botto Drust (2018), Donna McLean (2018), Denise Denis (2019), Lisa Denis (2020) and Beth Quesnel (2022).

Non-players inducted: owner Bill Simpson (1974), Joseph Barber (1975), Vincent Devitt (1976), John Pekar (1980), Anthony Caldaroni (1984), Bernie Kaplan (1986), John Stratton (1986), Jay Santoli (1995), Ralph Raymond (1996) and Bob Baird (2017).

BIBLIOGRAPHY

Books

Harrison, Pat. *North American Girls of Summer*. Qualicum Beach, BC: Pat Harrison, 2021.

Websites

Allyson Rioux Memorial Foundation. "About Allyson. http://riouxmemorialfoundation.blogspot.com.
Ann Liguori. www.annliguori.com.
Facebook. "Danni Kemp Cancer Support Group Page." https://www.facebook.com/groups/1101583899921424/?mibextid=6NoCDW.
The Fifth Estate. http://www.thefifthestateband.com.
International Women's Professional Softball. "Connecticut Falcons." https://sites.google.com/site/iwpsoftball/the-teams/connecticut-falcons?pli=1.
Michele Smith Fastpitch. michelesmith.com.
National Fastpitch Coaches Association. nfca.org.
Newspapers. newspapers.com.
Seven Angels Theatre. https://www.7atheatre.org.
Softball National News Past and Present. https://sites.google.com/site/softballnationalnews/home.
Stratford Connecticut's Women's Major Fastpitch Brakettes Softball. brakettes.com.
Team USA. "National Softball Hall of Fame." https://www.teamusa.org/usa-softball/national-softball-hall-of-fame.
Women in Softball. https://sites.google.com/site/womeninsoftball/.

Personal Communications

Blalock, Jane. Personal communications and email correspondence with author.
Chin, Debbie. Personal communications and email correspondence with author.

Compton, Joyce. Interview and personal communications with author, September 21, 2018.

Drust, Kristine Botto. Interview and personal communications with author.

Evans, Ken. Personal communications, email and phone correspondence with author.

Finelli, Linda. Interview and personal communications with author.

Gage, Harlan, and Kathy Gage. Personal communications and email correspondence with author.

Harrison, Pat. Personal communications and email correspondence with author.

Henderson, Danielle. Personal communications and email correspondence with author.

Hollis, Bev (Mulonet). Personal communications, email and phone correspondence with author.

Hutchins, Carol. Personal communications, email and phone correspondence with author.

Irwin, Stormy. Personal communications and email correspondence with author.

Joyce, Joan. Interview and personal communications with author, July 2, 2018, and numerous other dates.

Joyce, Joe, Jr. Interview and personal communications with author, December 3, 2018, and numerous other dates.

Kellers, Peggy. Personal communications and email correspondence with author.

King, Billie Jean. Email correspondence.

Ledbetter, Jackie. Personal communications and email correspondence with author.

Liguori, Ann. Personal communications and email correspondence with author.

Lopiano, Donna. Personal communications and email correspondence with author.

Morra, Marty. Personal communications and email correspondence with author.

Nelson, Janice. Personal communications, email and phone correspondence with author.

Pacelli, Paul. Personal communications and email correspondence with author.

Rienzi, Bill. Personal communications and email correspondence with author.

Santoli, Fran. Personal communications and email correspondence with author.

Schumacher, Diane. Personal communications and email correspondence with author.

Serafin, Pat. Personal communications and email correspondence with author.

Shea, Irene. Personal communications and email correspondence with author.

Smith, Michele. Personal communications, email and phone correspondence with author.

Strahan, Kathy. Personal communications and email correspondence with author.

Stratton, John. Personal communications and email correspondence with author.

Sutcliffe, Christina. Interview and personal communications with author, September 19, 2018.

Valentine, Bobby. Personal communications, email and phone correspondence with author.

Wright, Margie. Personal communications and email correspondence with author.

INDEX

ABOUT THE AUTHOR

Courtesy of Mary Ellen Blacker and Mary Renzoni.

Tony Renzoni is the author of the well-received books *Connecticut Rock 'n' Roll: A History*, *Connecticut Softball Legend Joan Joyce*, *Connecticut Bootlegger Queen Nellie Green* and *Historic Connecticut Music Venues: From the Coliseum to the Shaboo*.

Tony had a thirty-eight-year career with the federal government. As district manager in Connecticut's Fairfield County, he oversaw the operations of four field offices, serving over 100,000 beneficiaries. He wrote over one thousand weekly columns that were published in the *Connecticut Post* newspaper and on the paper's website. Tony was a recipient of more than forty awards, including his agency's highest honor award.

Renzoni serves as a consultant for the hit *Joan Joyce Musical*, which is based on his book *Connecticut Softball Legend Joan Joyce*.

A lifelong resident of Connecticut, Tony is a graduate of Sacred Heart High School in Waterbury and Sacred Heart University in Fairfield.

Other Books by Tony Renzoni

Connecticut Bootlegger Queen Nellie Green
Connecticut Rock 'n' Roll: A History
Connecticut Softball Legend Joan Joyce
Historic Connecticut Music Venues: From the Coliseum to the Shaboo

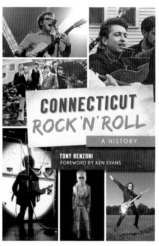

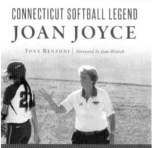
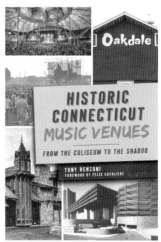